Ebenezer Lethbridge

An Easy Introduction to the History and Geography of Bengal

For the Junior Classes in Schools

Ebenezer Lethbridge

An Easy Introduction to the History and Geography of Bengal
For the Junior Classes in Schools

ISBN/EAN: 9783337178420

Printed in Europe, USA, Canada, Australia, Japan

Cover: Foto ©Paul-Georg Meister /pixelio.de

More available books at **www.hansebooks.com**

AN EASY INTRODUCTION

TO THE

HISTORY AND GEOGRAPHY OF BENGAL.

FOR THE JUNIOR CLASSES IN SCHOOLS.

BY

E. LETHBRIDGE, M.A.,

LATE SCHOLAR OF EXETER COLLEGE, OXFORD; OFFICIATING PRINCIPAL OF
KRISHNAGAR COLLEGE, BENGAL.

CALCUTTA:
THACKER, SPINK & CO.,
Publishers to the Calcutta University.
BOMBAY: THACKER, VINING & Co.   MADRAS: HIGGINBOTHAM & Co.
LONDON: W. THACKER AND CO.

1874.

CONTENTS.

		Page
CHAPTER I.—THE GEOGRAPHY OF BENGAL		1
,, II.—THE HINDU RULE IN BENGAL		10

,, III.—THE MUHAMMADAN RULE IN BENGAL :—
PART I.—The Governors of Lakhnautí under the Pathán Emperors of Dehli ... 17

,, IV.—DITTO :—
PART II.—The Independent Kings of Bengal 25

,, V.—DITTO :—
PART III.—The Dynasty of Sher Sháh ... 33

,, VI.—DITTO :—
PART IV.—The Mughul Súbahdárs under the Emperors of Dehli 41

,, VII.—DITTO :—
PART V.—The Nawábs of Bengal, nominally under the Emperors of Delhi, but really independent 75

,, VIII.—THE ENGLISH RULE IN BENGAL :—
PART I.—From the Battle of Plassey, 1757, to the Regulating Act, 1774 87

,, IX.—DITTO :—
PART II.—The Governors-General of British India as Governors of Bengal 97

PREFACE.

DURING the years that have elapsed since the preparation of the last *History of Bengal* that has issued from the press, fresh materials for such a work have rapidly accumulated. Many ancient historical works, then almost unknown, have recently been translated, or in other ways rendered accessible to the enquirer; hundreds, perhaps thousands, of inscriptions and coins have been read and interpreted by the art of the antiquarian; record-rooms have been ransacked, both in Calcutta and elsewhere; and as the result of all these researches, a flood of light has been thrown on many periods of Bengal history that twenty years ago seemed to be wrapped for ever in impenetrable mystery. In support of this statement, I need only refer to the published works of Professor Lassen, Bábu Rájendralála Mitra, and Mr. E. V. Westmacott, on the Hindú Period in Bengal; to those of Sir Henry Elliott, Professor Blochmann, Mr. E. Thomas, and Professor Dowson, on the Muhammadan Period; and to those of Dr. Hunter, Mr. Toynbee, the late Bábu Kissory Chand Mitra, and Mr. Westmacott, on the recent period of British rule in this province. All these works I have most carefully studied; and have made them, with Stewart's *History of Bengal* for the Muhammadan period, the basis of the little book which I now offer to the public. The chapter on the *Geography* is founded mainly on recent Administration Reports, supplemented by Professor Blochmann's admirable paper on the *Geography and History of Bengal*, lately published in the Asiatic Society's *Journal*.

I have prepared this little book especially for the use of the younger boys in our English-teaching schools; and have been most careful to use only the simplest and easiest language throughout. I have also endeavoured to make the account as pleasing as possible to youthful minds, by omitting all dry and uninteresting details, and by inserting a good many illustrative anecdotes and stories derived chiefly from Firishtah. I venture to think that stories like that of *Sultán Ghiyás-ud-dín and the Kázi* at p. 27, whilst they help to sustain the attention of young boys, are also often useful in other ways—sometimes by enabling the learner better to realise the scenes described in the historical account, sometimes by conveying valuable moral lessons.

E. L.

Krishnagar College,
July 1, 1874.

HISTORY AND GEOGRAPHY OF BENGAL.

CHAPTER I.

THE GEOGRAPHY OF BENGAL.

NOTE.—*This Chapter should be studied before a Map of the Lower Provinces.*

§ 1. Extent and Divisions. § 2. Bengal Proper. § 3. Bihár. § 4. Orissa. § 5. Chutiá Nágpur. § 6. Assam. § 7. The River System. § 8. Mountains and Hills. § 9. Plains. § 10. Lakes. § 11. Climate. § 12. Products. § 13. Manufactures. § 14. Races and Religions.

§ 1. *Extent and Divisions.*—The English name BENGAL was at one time given to nearly the whole of Northern India, which was called *The Presidency of Fort William in Bengal;* but it is now generally used to denote the country under the government of the Lieutenant-Governor of Bengal, which is sometimes called *The Lower Provinces of Bengal.* In the beginning of the year 1874, the great Province of Assam (which had formerly been included in the Lower Provinces) was separated from the rest of Bengal, and placed under the rule of the Chief Commissioner of Assam; but as this change is a very recent one, we shall speak of Assam as if it still formed a part of Bengal.

Bengal, then, comprises Bengal Proper, Bihár, Orissa, and Chutiá Nágpur, with some dependencies, governed by a Lieutenant-Governor; and Assam, with its dependencies, governed by a Chief Commissioner. These provinces lie between 19° 18′ and 28° 15′ north latitude, and between 82° and 97° east longitude; they contain about 250,000 square miles, and about sixty-seven millions of inhabitants.

§ 2. *Bengal Proper.*—Bengal Proper is a great plain lying between the Himálaya Mountains (the highest mountains in the world) and that part of the sea which is called the Bay of Bengal. It is intersected by a large number of rivers, branches either of the Ganges or the Brahmaputra; and its soil is for the most part the mud that has been brought down and deposited by these rivers. The language generally spoken is Bengáli; and the name of the country in that language is Bangálá or Banga-des, the country of Banga. It contains more than 94,000 square miles, and nearly 37,000,000 people. It is divided into six provinces or "Divisions," each under the rule of a Commissioner. There are three divisions in the middle, two on the east, and one on the west.

Of the three divisions in the middle, the southern one, next to the Bay of Bengal, is called the Presidency Division; because it contains Calcutta, which is called a "Presidency," because it was formerly the seat of government of an English President. At the junction of the Bhágirathí and the Jalangí rivers (both of which belong to the Ganges) is situated Nuddea, *Nadiyá*, or *Navadwípa*, formerly the Hindú capital of Bengal. It is in the zilá of Nuddea or Krishnagar, which is a part of the Presidency Division; and in the same zilá, higher up on the Bhágirathí river is Plassey (Palásí), the scene of the great battle in 1757 by which the English became masters of Bengal. The part of the Presidency Division, which is close to the sea, is a wild region of jungle and swamps, now called the *Sundarban*, and formerly called *Bhátí*. North of the Presidency Division, is the Rájsháhí Division; formerly called *Varendra*, and situated in the very midst of Bengal. In this division is Murshidábád, once the capital of the Muhammadan Nawábs of Bengal; and also, in the zilá now called Máldah, are the ruins of Gaur or Lakhnautí, once the Hindú capital of Bengal. North of the Rájsháhí Division, and stretching into the Himálaya Mountains, is the Division of Koch Bihár, in which is situated Dárjiling, a place possessing a very cool climate because it is high up on a mountain.

The two Divisions on the eastern side of Bengal are called Dacca *(Dháká)*, and Chittagong *(Chátgáon)*. In the Dacca

Division, near Náráyanganj, are the ruins of Sunárganw, formerly the capital of Eastern Bengal. The town of Dacca was called by the Muhammadans Jahángirnagar; and the town of Chittagong was called by them Islámábád.

The western Division of Bengal is called Bardwán, from the name of its chief town, which also gives name to an important zilá. This province was called Rárá by the Hindús in very ancient times; and lies to the west of the Bhágirathí or Hugli river. One of the five zilás of this Division is called Hugli; and in it, near the present town of Hugli, are the ruins of Sátganw, formerly the capital of Western Bengal.

§ 3. *Bihár.*—Bihár contains more than 42,000 square miles, and nearly 20,000,000 inhabitants. It is the plain on both sides of the Ganges, lying further up the river than Bengal, and between Bengal and the North-West Provinces. It consists of two great provinces or divisions; Bhágalpur or Eastern Bihár, and Patná or Western Bihár. The languages chiefly spoken are Hindí and Hindústání. Bihár was once the chief seat of the Buddhist religion; and it got its name (Sanskrit *Vihára*, a monastery) from the number of Buddhist monasteries which were formerly there.

One of the districts contained in the Division of Bhágalpur or Eastern Bihár, is called "the Santál Parganás," because it contains a large number of Santáls, an aboriginal tribe; and the people of another aboriginal tribe, called Pahárías, inhabit the Rájmahall Hills in the same district. *Rájmahall* is a town which was of considerable importance during the rule of the Mughuls in Bengal [*see* Chap. V., § 4, and Chap. VI. § 4]; it was built by Rájá Mán Singh, and was afterwards called Akbarnagar, in honour of the great emperor Akbar. At this place the last king of Bengal was defeated and killed by Akbar's army in 1576. North-west of Rájmahall, at the point where the Rájmahall Hills abut on the river Ganges, was the fortress of *Teliágarhí*, which used to be looked upon as the "Key" of Bengal [*see* Chap. V., § 4; Chap. VI., § 10].

The most important zilás of Patná or Western Bihár, are Patná, Tirhut, and Sháhábád. Patná was once called Pátaliputra (in Greek *Palibothra*), and was the capital of the ancient empire of Magadha. In Shábábád is situated Baxar (*Baksar*), where the English under Sir Hector Munro defeated Mír Kásim and the Vazír of Oudh in 1764; and in the same district are three other places of historical importance, of which we shall hear hereafter—*Chausá, Sahsarám*, and *Rahtás*. The country of Tirhut was formerly called Kosala; it is now one of the most populous districts in the world.

§ 4. *Orissa.*—Orissa contains nearly 24,000 square miles, and about four-and-a-half millions of inhabitants. It consists of a long flat strip of low-lying muddy land, the valleys of the river Mahánadí and of several smaller rivers between the Mahánadí and the Ganges; together with a wild hilly region in the interior of the country. It lies south-west of Bengal, between the mountains on the west and the Bay of Bengal on the east. The language spoken most generally is Uriyá; but in the hilly country there are many aboriginal tribes (such as the Khands and others) who speak different dialects. Under the Hindú rule, Orissa was called Odra or Utkalá.

Southern Orissa is called the zilá or district of Púrí, famous for the temples of Jagannáth, which are visited by thousands of pilgrims at the festival called *Rath Játrá*. Central Orissa is called Cuttack (Katak); it contains the towns of *Katak Banáras* (on the right bank of the Mahánadí), and *Jájpur*—which have been at various times the capitals of Orissa. The district of Balasor, or north-east Orissa, is watered by the Subarnarekha and the Baitaraní, two rivers which rise in Chutiá Nágpur and flow southward through Orissa into the Bay of Bengal.

§ 5. *Chutiá Nágpur.*—Chutiá Nágpur or Hazáríbágh, formerly called *Jhárkhand*, is a mountainous district lying west of Bengal Proper and Bihár, north of Orissa, and east of the Central Provinces. It is called *Chutiá* Nágpur, from Chutiá, a town near Ránchi. Many of its inhabitants belong to aboriginal tribes:—such as the *Kols*, divided into *Oraons* and *Mundás*; the *Santáls*; and others. Of the many rivers that rise in Chutiá Nágpur, some flow northward and eastward to join the Ganges; others flow southward through Orissa into the Bay of Bengal; and others flow, also southward, to join the Mahánadí. The total area of the province is nearly 44,000 square miles; and its population nearly four millions. Attached to it are many petty States whose chiefs pay a tribute to the British Government, and refer the judicial decision of very serious cases to the Commissioner, but who in other matters administer the government themselves. These petty States are called *Tributary Mahalls*; and there are also many such petty States attached to the province of Orissa.

§ 6. *Assam*.—Assam consists of the long valley of the Brahmaputra, with many adjacent hill-tracts. It contains an area of more than 43,000 square miles; and a population of two millions and a quarter. Western Assam, including the adjacent parts of northeast Bengal, was formerly called *Kámrúp*. The language generally spoken is Assamese, very much like the Bengáli; but there are many hill-tribes who speak quite different languages. The northern banks of the Brahmaputra are called Uttarkol; and the southern banks, Dakhinkol.

The name *Assam* is derived from the *Ahoms*, an aboriginal tribe that ruled in Upper Assam for four and a half centuries. The Ahoms are still numerous in the province, and are now scarcely different from the ordinary Hindús in manners and religion, except that they have priests of their own, who are called *Bilongs*.

§ 7. *The River System*.—The river system of Bengal is of very great importance, because the rivers in this country generally serve for roads; and most of the internal commerce is carried on by means of boats on the rivers which traverse all parts of the country. The chief rivers of the province are:—

(a). The *Ganges*, which enters Bengal from the North-Western Provinces near Ghazipur. Shortly afterwards it receives the waters of the Ghogra on its left or north side, then the Son on its south side, and then the Ghandak again on its north side at Hájipur, opposite Patná. These three tributaries are all large rivers; and the Ganges throughout this part of its course has generally an easterly direction. Below Bhágalpur it is joined by another great tributary, the Kúsí; after which it turns southward around the corner of the Rájmahall Hills, and continues in that direction until it divides into two great streams,—of which one, flowing to the south-east to Goalando, retains the name of Ganges; whilst the other, flowing to the south-west towards Hugli and Calcutta, is called at first the *Bhágirathí*, and afterwards the *Hugli*.

(*b*). The *Brahmaputra* is formed by the union of many large streams that rise on the northern and eastern slopes of the Himálayas; it enters Assam at its north-east corner, and flows through the whole length of the Assam valley. It then skirts the Gáro Hills, and flows due south to meet the main stream of the Ganges near Goalando. The united rivers flow by many mouths into the Bay of Bengal.

[NOTE.—The country lying between the mouths of a river is called its *Delta*. The delta formed by the Ganges and the Brahmaputra is a very large one, and includes the whole of the Presidency Division, and parts of the Rájsháhí and Dacca Divisions, of Bengal Proper.]

(*c*). The *Mahánadí* is the chief river of Orissa. It rises in the Central Provinces; and flows through Orissa into the Bay of Bengal in a generally south-easterly direction. Most of the low country of Orissa is comprised within the delta of this great river. It is about 520 miles in length, and is navigable for boats for 460 miles; near Cuttack *(Katak)* it is about two miles in breadth.

(*d*). The other rivers of Bengal are of less importance. The *Surmá* flows past Silhat, and is the high road to Kachár; it joins the Brahmaputra, and the united rivers are then called the Megna. The two rivers of the Chittagong Division are, the *Phaní* (or Fenny River), which separates Chittagong from Tiparah; and the *Karnphulí*, on which Chittagong itself is situated.

The rivers of the Bardwán Division are, the *Damudár*, which flows through Bardwán itself; the *Rúpnáráin*, which flows through Bánkurá; and the *Kasai*, which flows through Midnapur. All these join the Hugli between Calcutta and Ságar Island, where it falls into the sea.

Besides the Mahánadí, Orissa has two other rivers; the *Baitarani*, which flows into the Bay of Bengal near Point Palmyras;

and the Subarnarekhá, which passes by Jellasor. Both these rivers rise in Chutiá Nágpur, and flow through Orissa in a south-easterly direction.

§ 8. *Mountains and Hills.*—A small part of the great Himálaya Range, the loftiest chain of mountains in the world, is situated within the territories of Lower Bengal. The elevation of these mountains varies greatly—from Dárjiling in the south, 7,000 feet above the level of the sea, to Kachinjanga on the north-west, 28,000 feet. The highest peak of the Himálaya Mountains is in Nepál,—*viz.*, Mount Everest, 29,000 feet.

The Rájmahall Hills are in Eastern Bihár, and are an eastern projection of the mountainous country of Central India. The whole of Chutiá Nágpur is hilly, and much of it is a very high table-land. Between this plateau and the Rájmahall Hills are numerous detached mountains rising almost abruptly from the plains; of these the highest is *Parisnáth*, above 4,500 feet, the sacred hill of the Jains.

The interior of Orissa is hilly, and covered with rocks and jungle. The highest groups are the mountains of Keonjhar and Talchír.

In Eastern Bengal and Assam there are numerous ranges of hills, stretching under various names from the north-east corner of Assam to the south of the Chittagong Division. Those north of the Brahmaputra are called from the tribes inhabiting them, the *Aká, Duphla, Mírí* and *Mishmi Hills*; and are merely outer ranges of the great Himálaya Mountains. Of those south of the Brahmaputra, farthest to the north-east are the Abor and Singphú Hills; then the Nágá Hills to the south of the Assam valley, which are connected by the Manipur, Kachár, and Tiparah Hills, with the Chittagong Hill Tracts; whilst the range of the Gáro and Khasiá and Jaintiá Hills runs parallel to the Himálayas as far as the bend of the Brahmaputra.

§ 9. *Plains.*—The greater part of Bengal and Bihár is an uninterrupted flat, subject to inundation, rich in black mould, and highly productive; some portions are more fertile than others, the Dacca Division being so fertile as to be called the granary of Bengal. In the eastern portion of this plain the soil is muddy, and the climate humid; in the western part, the soil more resembles that of the Chutiá Nágpur plateau, containing granite and sometimes coal, and the climate is somewhat drier.

The Assam Valley is almost a perfect flat, with clumps of little conical hills scattered over the plain and rising abruptly to the height of 200 to 700 feet. A large number of rivers flow through this plain to join the Brahmaputra, the soil is particularly rich in minerals, and the climate is very favourable to the growth of the tea-plant.

§ 10. *Lakes.*—There is a large salt lake close to the coast on the southern border of Orissa, called the Chilká Lake, into which some branches of the Mahánadí flow. Besides this, there are numerous shallow lakes called *jhils* in various parts of Bengal, of which the water is generally brackish.

§ 11. *Climate.*—The climate of the greater part of Bengal is generally hot and moist; in the hills, and especially in the highlands of Kachár and Assam, an enormous quantity of rain falls every year. During the rainy season, the climate of Hazáribágh is much cooler than that of the rest of Bengal; in the Himálaya Mountains (at Darjíling for instance) the climate is cool throughout the year.

From about February to November the summer *monsoon* prevails,—*i.e.*, the wind generally blows from the sea over the land, from south or south-west to north. During the rest of the year the winter monsoon blows, from the north and north-west toward the Bay of Bengal. Terrific storms, called *cyclones*, (because the wind whirls about in a circle as the storm sweeps over the country), sometimes occur during the summer monsoon; and especially at the beginning and at the end, about the change of the monsoons. Other storms of considerable violence, though not so destructive as cyclones, frequently occur in the hot-weather; these generally blow from the north-west, and are called in English "north-westers."

§ 12. *Products.*—The principal food-grain of Bengal Proper is rice, which is most largely produced in Eastern and Central Bengal, and in Orissa. There are two chief crops of rice,—

the *aus*, harvested in July and September; and the *áman* or winter-crop, harvested in December and January.

In Bihár also, rice is the most important food-grain; but a great deal of wheat, maize, barley, peas, and other grains are also grown and eaten.

Millets of various kinds, *marwá*, and maize, are the staple food of the lowest classes in Chutiá Nágpur.

The chief commercial productions of Bengal are jute *(pát)*, grown largely in Eastern Bengal, chiefly for exportation; and cocoa-nuts, betel-nuts, plantains and other fruits and vegetables, bamboos, and thatch-grass, chiefly for sale in the province. *Ganjah* or hemp, *mushina* or flax, oil-seeds, sugar-cane, and date-sugar, are largely produced in most parts of the country. Tea is largely cultivated in Assam (where also some cotton is produced), in Kachár and Sikkim, and to some extent in Chittagong; whilst silk and lac are exported from the central districts and from Chútiá Nágpur. Indigo is largely grown in Bihár, north of the Ganges. Opium is only allowed to be grown for the Government, chiefly in Bihár.

§ 13. *Manufactures.*—Indigo is largely manufactured in the Presidency, Rájshábí, Bardwán and Dacca Divisions, and in East and West Bihár; opium in West Bihár; silk in Rájshábí and Bardwán; sugar in the Presidency Division; salt in Orissa.

§ 14. *Races and Religions.*—The races of Bengal are more varied than those of any other part of India. The bulk of the population consists of Aryan Hindús, with a large admixture of aboriginal tribes in the lower castes; the Kayasthas are the most numerous and important caste, and inferior in rank only to Bráhmans. The Muhammadans are most numerous in South Eastern Bengal; many of them are descendants of the old Afghán conquerors of Bengal, [*see* Chap. II.], and a few are Mughuls; but large numbers are converts from low Hindú, aboriginal, and Arakanese tribes.

The aboriginal tribes, besides forming a considerable portion of the lowest classes on the plains, are chiefly found in the hill-districts of Assam, Eastern Bengal, Chutiá Nágpur, Orissa, and Eastern Bíhár. The chief divisions of these tribes are the

Lohitic, the *Kolarian*, and the *Dravidian* races. To the Lohitic race belong most of the tribes of Assam and Sikkim, as the Mishmís, Duphlás, Gáros, Nágás, Kachárís, Jaintiás, Lúshais, Kúkís, and Lepchas. To the Kolarian race belong the Kols, Santáls, and others. To the Dravidian race belong the Khands in Orissa, and the Rájmahall Paháriás.

Altogether there are, in the Lower Provinces, about 31½ millions of Hindús, 21 millions of Muhammadans, and 14 millions of aborigines.

CHAPTER II.

THE HINDU RULE IN BENGAL.

§ 1. The Aryan Invasion. § 2. Legendary character of the early history. § 3. The Lords Paramount of India. § 4. Buddhism and Bráhmanism. § 5. The earliest Dynasties in Bengal. § 6. The Pál Dynasty. § 7. The Sena Dynasty and King Adisúra. § 8. King Ballála Sena. § 9. The last Hindú Kings of Bengal. § 10. The remains of the Hindú Power in Bengal. § 11. The Early History of Assam. § 12. The Early History of Orissa.

§ 1. *The Aryan Invasion.*—Many hundreds of years ago, it is believed that all Bengal was occupied by the aboriginal tribes mentioned in the last paragraph, the Kols, Santáls, and others. At last the Bráhmanical Hindús, who had conquered the Panjáb and the rest of Upper India, penetrated into Bengal; they subdued the earlier possessors, and drove them away to the hills and jungles, or reduced them to slavery. Now these Hindús, whom I have called *Bráhmanical* because their priests were called Bráhmans, were a branch of a mighty nation called the Aryans, who had formerly lived in Central Asia, before they came to India. This branch of the Aryan race was the ancestor of the modern Hindús of the higher classes; and other branches of the same race migrated westward from Central Asia into Europe, and became the ancestors of the English, the French, the Germans, and most of the other peoples of Europe.

When this Aryan invasion took place is not known exactly; but after this, and for many hundreds of years—indeed until the Muhammadan conquest in A.D. 1203—Bengal was ruled by Aryan Hindú princes.

§ 2. *Legendary character of the early history.*—There has been no trustworthy account preserved by the Hindús of those ancient times when Bengal was ruled by native Hindús; the stories that are contained in the Puránas, or that have been handed down by tradition, are generally of a poetical or legendary character. But some knowledge of the true history has been obtained from inscriptions that have been found in various parts of the country, cut on stone or metal in those ancient times, and legible even at the present day. Moreover the Muhammadans, who were very fond of writing history, shortly after their conquest of Bengal, wrote down all that was then remembered about the ancient history; and in these and other ways we have now got to know something about those obscure ages.

§ 3. *The Lords Paramount of India.*—In the early times before the Muhammadan conquest, India was divided into a very large number of Hindú kingdoms and principalities, some large and powerful, others small and weak. These were generally independent; but sometimes one of the kings or princes conquered all or most of the rest, and then he assumed the title of *Mahárájá Adhiráj*, or Lord Paramount of India.

It is thought by some that at least one of the early kings of Bengal, a powerful prince named Deva Pál, obtained the title of Mahárájá Adhiráj; and at other times it is probable that the kings of Bengal were occasionally subordinate to other princes who held the title. Thus, about 2,200 years ago, and for many centuries after that time, Bengal and Orissa were subordinate parts of a great empire whose capital was in Bihár. This was the empire of Magadha; and its capital was called Pátaliputra (or Palibothra by the Greeks), the modern Patna.

§ 4. *Buddhism and Bráhmanism.*—The Emperors of Magadha, with most of their subjects, had ceased to profess the religion of the Bráhmanical Hindús, and followed quite a different religion, called Buddhism. The great king Asoka was the first Buddhist

Emperor of Magadha (B.C. 263—223); and edicts or laws, engraved on stones by the orders of Asoka, have been found in Orissa, as well as in many other distant parts of India.

This new religion was the chief religion of India for at least a thousand years—after which the kings and their peoples gradually turned to a somewhat altered form of their original religion. This later form is generally called Bráhmanism or Hindúism; and is essentially the same religion as that professed at the present day by most Hindús.

§ 5. *Earliest Dynasties in Bengal.*—It is probable that, of the earliest kings of Bengal, some were subject to the Mauryan Kings of Magadha, of whom Asoka was the most famous; others at a later period were subject to the Andhra Kings, who had obtained power in Magadha; others again still later were probably subject to the kings of Kashmír, and after that to the kings of Kanauj. But of these early kings we know absolutely nothing further.

§ 6. *The Pál Dynasty.*—At length, about the year 700 A.D., a good and powerful king named *Bhu Pál* came to the throne, who, though a Buddhist, was kind to people of the Hindú religion; and he was the first of a powerful dynasty of about twelve kings who reigned in succession, all of whom were called Pál, and were Buddhists in religion. The third king of this line was called *Deva Pál;* I have already said of him that it is believed he conquered many neighbouring princes, and became *Mahárájá Adhirája* [see § 3]. And many years afterwards, about 913 A.D., one of his descendants named *Mahi Pál* greatly distinguished himself as a wise and good ruler; he made large and splendid tanks, some of which (such as the Mahipáldighi in Dinájpur) still exist and bear his name.

§ 7. *The Sena Dynasty, and King Adisúra.*—The circumstances under which the Pál dynasty ceased to reign in Bengal are unknown; but it appears likely that they were displaced by a revolution in which the supporters of the Hindú or Bráhmanical religion subverted Buddhism. At any rate, the Páls were succeeded by a dynasty of kings called *Sena,* who were ardent supporters of Bráhmanism. One of the most famous of these was called Adisúra; and he was probably the founder of the Sena family, and became king about A.D. 964.

Now, during the centuries of Buddhist rule in Bengal, it is likely that many of the doctrines and rites of the Bráhmanical religion had been forgotten. So king Adisúra determined to fetch some Bráhman sages from those parts of India where the Buddhist religion had never entirely overridden Hindúism. The only city in which the Bráhmans had continuously retained their influence was Kanauj (*Kanyakubja*) on the borders of Oudh, in the modern division of Agra. There the Bráhmanical rites had never been forgotten; so King Adisúra sent to Kanauj, and brought thence five learned Bráhmans—Bhattanáráyana, Daksha, Srí Harsha, Chhándada, and Vedagarbha. These five sages came, each attended by a Káyastha; and these are said to be the ancestors of the five high classes of Bráhmans and Káyasthas in Bengal.

§ 8. *King Ballála Sena.*—The greatest of all the Sena kings, the descendants of Adisúra, was Ballála Sena. His father Vijaya Sena had been a great conqueror; and had invaded Kámrúp or West Assam, and Kalinga the country on the coast of the Bay of Bengal, south of Orissa. Ballála Sena came to the throne about the year 1066 A.D., exactly the time of the Norman Conquest in England, when a son of the great Mahmúd of Ghazní was reigning in the Panjáb. Ballála was a wise and powerful monarch, and a great patron of learning, being himself an author. He reigned thirty-five years; and to his wisdom and valour are assigned a great number of exploits and reforms, some of which doubtless belong to him, whilst others are assigned to him only because he was the most famous prince of the period. Amongst other fables that were invented to account for his greatness, it was said that his father was really not Vijaya Sena, but the god of the river Brahmaputra. His chief residence was Rámpant in the Dacca district; but he subsequently built a capital near Gaur in the district of Máldah, and called it Lakhnautí (contracted from Lakshmanavatí) after his son Lakshmana.

But the most famous act of king Ballála Sena was the classification of the descendants of the Bráhmans and Káyasthas who had been brought from Kanauj by Adisura. Ballála finally settled their rank; and this was the origin of *Kulinism* (*kula*). In Ballála's time, Bengal was divided into five provinces; and the five orders of Bráhmans and Káyasthas took their distinctive names from these provinces. They were (1) *Rárá*, the country west of the Hugli and south of the Ganges; (2) *Bágri*, the delta of the Ganges; (3) *Banga*, the country to the east of, and beyond the delta; (4) *Varendra*, the country to the north of the Poddah (*Padmá*) and between the Karatayá and Mahánandá rivers; and (5) *Mithilá*, the country west of the Mahánandá. These divisions correspond to some extent with the modern divisions [*see* Chap. I.]; Rárá corresponding in part with the Bardwán Division; Bágri with the Presidency Division; Banga with the Dacca and Chittagong Divisions; Varendra with the Rájsháhí Division; and Mithilá with Bihár.

§ 9. *The last Hindú Kings of Bengal.*—Lakshmana Sena succeeded his father Ballála about the year 1101. Some inscriptions that have been discovered state that he erected pillars of victory at Benares, Allahábád, and Jagannáth (or Púrí in Orissa); but all that is known of him is that he greatly beautified the city of Lakhnautí.

Lakshmana Sena died in 1121; and was followed successively by his two sons Mádhava Sena and Kesava Sena. The last Hindú King of Bengal is called by the Hindús, Su Sen or Sura Sen; by the Muhammadan historians he is called Lakhmaniyá; and he reigned for eighty years, from A.D. 1123 to A.D. 1203. The Muhammadan historian says of him. "He was a liberal man, and never gave less than a lakh of cowries when he made a present; may God lessen his punishment in hell!"

Lakhmaniyá lived at Nadiyá in great luxury; and in his old age was not at all likely to be able to withstand the attacks of the Muhammadans, who had now conquered Dehli and most of the kings of Northern India. When news was brought that Bakhtyár Khiljí and his Muhammadans had subdued Bihár and were approaching, the Bráhmans and astrologers informed Lakhmaniyá that a prophecy had declared that his kingdom was to be subverted at this very time by the Turks; and they begged the

Rájá to remove his people and wealth to the remote districts of the east, where they would be safe from attack. They added, in reply to the prince's questions, that the length of Bakhtyár Khiljí's arms proved that he was the conqueror referred to in the prophecy. Lakhmaniyá however refused to leave his comfortable palace at Nadiyá; so the nobles and principal inhabitants left him and fled, some to Banga, others to Orissa. Next year, the long-armed Muhammadan soldier surprised old Lakhmaniyá in his palace; and the latter escaped with the greatest difficulty, and fled with hardly any attendants to Jagannáth in Orissa. In this holy spot he shortly afterwards died.

§ 10. *The remains of the Hindú Power in Bengal.*—The regular line of the old Hindú kings of Bengal ended with Lakhmaniyá; but his relatives and their followers maintained the Hindú power in Eastern and Southern Bengal, and it was about a hundred years before Banga and the southern portions of Rárá and Bágri were brought thoroughly under Muhammadan rule.

§ 11. *Early History of Assam.*—The inhabitants of Assam were at all times objects of dread to the more civilised kingdoms in Bengal; and though we often hear of invasions of Kámrúp, and some of the south-western part of the country was ultimately conquered by the Mughuls in 1637 (Silhat was annexed to Bengal in 1384), yet during the Hindú period and the early Muhammadan period Eastern Bengal was frequently overrun by Assamese.

In early times the *Chutiyá* tribe was the ruling power, both in Upper and Lower Assam; and many descendants of this tribe are still to be found there. But about the time of the Muhammadan conquest of Bengal, the Chutiyás were conquered by the *Koch* in Lower Assam and by the *Ahoms* in Upper Assam; and the Ahoms ultimately became the masters of the whole country.

§ 12. *Early History of Orissa.*—Orissa was one of those countries in which Buddhism was adopted at a very early period, very shortly after the death of its founder. In the third century before Christ, Orissa formed a part of the empire of the great Buddhist king of Magadha or Bihár, Asoka; and many memorials of the Buddhist rule, in the form of carvings and inscriptions, are still to be found in the country.

Buddhism was predominant in Orissa until the expulsion of the *Yavana* dynasty in 473 A.D.; and it seems probable that most of the Yavana kings, who are generally represented as successful invaders from Bihár or from the sea, were Buddhists. During the period of Yavana or foreign rule, the island of Java was colonised by settlers from the shores of Orissa.

In 473 A.D., the Yavanas were finally expelled by a chief who professed the Bráhmanical religion, named *Yayáti Kesari*; and from this time Buddhism declined in Orissa, and the religion of the country became Hindú, at first Sivaism. Bhuvaneswar became the temple-city of Siva, as it had formerly been a home of Buddhism, and as Púri afterwards became a sanctuary of Vishnu. Jájpur also was the head-quarters of the Sivaite priesthood; and it was the capital of the country in the sixth century. For forty-three generations the Kesari dynasty ruled in Orissa; and the Lion-race (as it was called) was not expelled until 1132 A.D.

A warlike prince of this dynasty, named Makar Kesari, in the tenth century, built Cuttack (Katak); and this city has ever since been the capital of the country.

About the beginning of the 12th century, an invader named Chor-gangá got the better of the last king of the Kesari dynasty; and when the latter died without children, Chor-gangá succeeded him. The dynasty thus founded in 1132 A.D. lasted until only a few years before the Muhammadan conquest in 1567; it was called the Gangá Vansa, or Gangetic Race. The religion of the country now became Vishnuvite; some legends say that a period of Sun-worship intervened between the decline of Siva-worship and the establishment of Vaishnavism, and that a line of kings, called the Sun Dynasty, ruled from 655 A.D. to 1324 A.D.

The great temple of Jagannáth was built by the fourth monarch of the Gangá Vansa, in 1175—1198; and we have seen that, very shortly afterwards, in 1203 A.D., Lakhmaniyá the last Hindu king of Bengal fled to this sanctuary and died in its sacred shade.

Rájá Pratáp Chandra Deo was the last of the Gangá Vansa princes. His reign, from A.D. 1504—1532, is famous as the period when the great reformer, Chaitanya of Nadiyá, preached purity of religion throughout Orissa—converting even the king himself.

CHAPTER III.

THE MUHAMMADAN RULE IN BENGAL. PART I.—THE GOVERNORS OF LAKHNAUTI UNDER THE PATHAN EMPERORS OF DELHI.

From A.D. 1203 to A.D. 1338.

§ 1. Divisions of the Muhammadan Period of Bengal History. § 2. The Muhammadan Conquest of Dehli. § 3. Bakhtyár Khiljí, and the Muhammadan Conquest of Bengal. § 4. Bakhtyár Khiljí, the first Muhammadan king of Bengal. § 5. The Khiljí successors of Bakhtyár. § 6. Tughán Khán and Tughral Khán. § 7. Sultán Mughís-ud-dín Tughral. § 8. Bughrá Khán, and the Balbaní dynasty. § 9. The Balbaní dynasty continued; Bahádur Sháh. § 10. The Governors of Bengal under Muhammad bin Tughlaq.

§ 1. *Divisions of the Muhammadan Period of Bengal History.*—The history of Bengal under Muhammadan rule may be conveniently divided into five periods:—

1. The reigns of the Governors of Lakhnautí appointed by the Pathán Emperors of Dehli; from the conquest of Bengal by Muhammad Bakhtyár Khiljí in A.D. 1203, to the establishment of the independence of Bengal in A.D. 1338.

2. The reigns of the independent kings of Bengal; from A.D. 1338 to A.D. 1538.

3. The reigns of Sher Sháh and his Afghán successors; from A.D. 1538 to A.D. 1576.

4. The rule of the Súbahdárs of the Mughul Emperors of Dehli; from A. D. 1576 to A.D. 1740.

5. The rule of the Nawábs of Bengal, nominally subject to the Empire of Dehli, but really independent; from A.D. 1740 to the battle of Plassey in A.D. 1757.
The present chapter treats of the first period.

§ 2. *The Muhammadan Conquest of Dehli.*—The Afgháns and Túrks of Afghánistán, and the countries adjacent to it in Central Asia, had been converted to the Muhammadan religion at a very early period; and had frequently invaded the north-west of India, partly with the view of conquering it, and partly with the hope of extending the Muhammadan religion. The great Sultán of Ghazní, called Mahmúd, in the eleventh century, was the leader of some of the most successful of these invasions; but none of them ever reached as far eastward as Bengal.

At last, a great Muhammadan leader, called Shaháb-ud-dín or Muhammad Ghori (he was named *Ghori* because he was the Chief of Ghor, a small State in Afghánistán), conquered the Hindú king of Dehli and all his allies in the battle of Thaneswar, A.D. 1193; and Muhammad Ghori became the first Muhammadan Sultán of Dehli.

§ 3. *Bakhtyár Khiljí and the Muhammadan Conquest of Bengal.*—Muhammad Ghori did not himself attempt to complete the conquest of Northern India; but he lived chiefly in his native country, Afghánistán, and left the care of the wars in India to his chief commanders. One of these, named Kutb-ud-dín, completed the conquest of the North-West Provinces, Oudh, and part of Rájpútáná; and ultimately succeeded Muhammad Ghori as Sultán of Dehli.

Whilst Muhammad Ghori was living in Afghánistán, and Kutb-ud-dín was his viceroy or lieutenant in Dehli, a young Afghán leader, named Muhammad Bakhtyár, of the Khiljí tribe, greatly distinguished himself with the Muhammadan army then in Oudh. Getting together a few followers, he used to make plundering incursions into Bihár, which was still under the Hindú princes of Magadha; who then lived in the town of Bihár, but were not brave and powerful as Asoka and the ancient kings of Magadha had been. Bakhtyár Khiljí acquired great wealth in these plundering expeditions, and expended it in paying more followers;

and at last he succeeded in taking the town and fort of Bihár itself, which was at that time famous as a great seat of Hindú learning. The booty found here was very rich, and he gave it all to Kutb-ud-dín, the viceroy of Dehli; and obtained in consequence so many honours from Kutb that all the courtiers were jealous of him.

An interesting story is told about the jealousy of these courtiers. They treacherously proposed that Bakhtyár should exhibit his valour and skill before the viceroy, by encountering single-handed one of those terrible elephants that were kept in those days for the purpose of making sport by fighting with tigers or with other elephants. To their astonishment, Bakhtyár quietly girded up his loins and advancing to meet the enfuriated elephant, struck it such a blow on the trunk with his battle-axe that it ran away, pursued by the triumphant hero.

After this exploit, Bakhtyár rose higher than ever in public estimation and in the favour of the viceroy; and he was allowed to return to Bihár with a strong army, and with permission to conquer all the surrounding Hindú territories. After he had consolidated his possession of Bihár, he determined to attempt the conquest of Bengal; and he was encouraged to do this, by the accounts of the weakness and old age of Lakhmaniyá [see Chap. II., § 9]. He marched from Bihár towards Nadiyá very rapidly and very secretly, so that no one was aware of his approach; and hiding his army in the jungle near Nadiyá, he advanced to the city with only seventeen followers. Pretending that he was only an ambassador from another Rájá, he was allowed to enter and approach the palace; when he and his followers suddenly drew their swords, and commenced to slaughter the attendants of Lakhmaniyá. The Rájá fled; and the rest of the Muhammadan army coming up, Bakhtyár Khiljí easily became master of the city.

By this campaign he obtained possession of the whole of Bengal except the eastern and southern districts (*i.e.*, except Bangá and the southern portions of Rárá and Bágri; see Chap. II., § 10), A.D. 1203.

§ 4. *Bakhtyár Khiljí, the first Muhammadan King of Bengal.*—
The dominions of Bakhtyár Khiljí were divided into two pro-

vinces. Lakhnautí (where he fixed the royal residence, for he destroyed the Hindú city of Nadiyá) was the capital of the western province, which consisted of parts of Rárá or Bardwán, and Mithilá or Bihár. Deokot, near the modern Dinájpur, was the capital of the eastern province, which consisted of Varendra or Rájshábí, and a part of Bágri or Presidency. During the early part of his reign he devoted himself to the settlement of this province; and he founded Rangpur as a fortress to defend the country against the Hindús of the north. He appears also to have received as allies or as tributaries the Hindú Rájás of Lakhmaniyá's family who retained possession of Banga and the eastern districts.

At length, relying on the assistance of these friendly Hindús, and especially on the aid of a Rájá of the Koch tribe (living either in Koch Bihár or in Lower Assam) who had become a Musalmán, he determined to invade the Himálayan territories of Assam and Thibet. He crossed the Brahmaputra, but met with many disasters; and being forced to retreat, he was attacked by the Rájá of Kámrúp as he was recrossing the river, and was compelled to fly with only a few attendants, his whole army being cut off. He only survived this disgrace a short time; and one report states that he was murdered by one of his ambitious officers, who after a short interval succeeded to the throne of Bengal.

§ 5. *The Khiljí Successors of Bakhtyár.*—After the death of Muhammad Bakhtyár Khiljí, much anarchy prevailed for several years; and the most powerful officers of his army, who belonged to the Khiljí tribe, became successively Governors of Lakhnautí. The last and most powerful of these was Sultán *Ghiyás-ud-dín* Khiljí. He built a famous road through his dominions from Lakhnur in Bírbhúm to Lakhnautí, and thence to Deokot in Dinájpur; he also greatly improved the city of Lakhnautí, and decorated it with splendid buildings. He was a wise ruler both in peace and war; for he distributed justice with impartiality alike to Muhammadans and Hindús, and he compelled the Rájás of Kámrúp (Assam) and Jájpur (Orissa) to pay him tribute. The great Altamsh, who at this time was Emperor of horse into the stream; and Malik, plunging into the water, dragged him to the shore, and cut off his head. The Emperor Balban subsequently tarnished the glory of this valorous exploit of his followers, by cruelly slaughtering a large number of the adherents of Tughral in cold blood, *with their wives and children*, A.D. 1282.

§ 8. *Bughrá Khán, and the Balbaní Dynasty.*—Balban now appointed his second son Bughrá Khán Governor of Bengal with the title of Defender of the Faith (Násir-ud-dín). By the death of his elder brother, Bughrá Khán became heir to the empire, and was begged by Balban to come back to Dehli; but he preferred his quiet and secure rule in Bengal, and ultimately his eldest son Kaikubád became emperor, whilst Bughrá himself remained at Lakhnautí as king of Bengal.

A wicked and ambitious Vazír or minister of the emperor Kaikubád, named Nizám-ud-dín, endeavoured to sow discord between the father and son, because Bughrá Khán had warned his son against the machinations of the wicked Vazír, and had remonstrated with Kaikubád about his licentious habits. The result was that the father and son met, each at the head of an army, in the plains of Bihár. For two days the armies remained encamped near each other; on the third day, the old king of Bengal wrote a letter to his son with his own hand, begging for an interview. At first the wicked Vazír succeeded in preventing this interview; and even when it was arranged, he persuaded the weak young Kaikubád that it was necessary for his dignity as emperor of Hindústán, that his father the king of Bengal should first prostrate himself three times before him. At length the time for the meeting arrived. The son proceeded first to the Darbár tents with great pomp; then the aged father approached slowly, and as soon as he came in sight of the throne, made his first prostration: as he came nearer, he made the second prostration; and when he arrived at the foot of the throne, was about to make the third; when the prince, deeply affected at the humiliation of his father, and stung with remorse at his own undutiful conduct, rushed into the old man's arms; and after tenderly embracing him and imploring his forgiveness, forced him to sit on the throne whilst he himself took a respectful place below. The designs of the wicked Vazír were thus frustrated, and he shortly afterwards died by poison.

Bughrá Khán after this reigned peaceably in Bengal until his death, A.D. 1292; but his unfortunate son Kaíkubád was deposed and assassinated in 1290, by Jalál-ud-dín, the first emperor of the Khiljí dynasty. For the thirty years during which this dynasty was ruling in Dehli, the Balbaní dynasty (as Bughrá Khán, son of Balban, and his descendants were called) reigned in Bengal with little or no interference on the part of the Emperors of Hindústán.

§ 9. *The Balbaní Dynasty continued; Bahádur Sháh.*—The two younger sons of Bughrá Khán, named Kai Káús and Fíruz Sháh, reigned successively; and the two sons of the latter, Shaháb-ud-dín and Bahádúr Sháh (who were consequently grandsons of Bughrá Khán), appear to have divided Bengal between them, Shaháb-ud-dín being king of Lakhnautí, and Bahádúr Sháh king of Sunárganw. After a time Bahádur Sháh expelled his elder brother from Lakhnautí; and Shaháb-ud-dín sought the aid of Ghiyás-ud-din Tughlaq, the first of the Tughlaq Emperors, who in the meantime had driven out the Khiljí dynasty from the imperial throne of Dehli. The Emperor Ghiyás-ud-dín marched into Bengal, reinstated Shaháb-ud-dín as king, and carried off Bahádúr Sháh as a captive to Dehli.

But immediately after the accession of the second Emperor of the Tughlaq dynasty, Muhammad bin Tughlaq, to the throne of Dehli in 1325, he reinstated Bahádúr Sháh as king of Bengal. Bahádúr, however, who was of a turbulent disposition, did not long remain submissive to the Dehli Emperor. He began to issue coin in his own name, and to use the white umbrella which was the sign of independent sovereignty; so in the year 1333, Muhammad bin Tughlaq marched into Bengal and defeated and slew Bahádúr Sháh, whose skin stuffed with straw was sent to all the provinces of India as a warning to refractory Governors.

§ 10. *The Governors of Bengal under Muhammad bin Tughlaq.*—Bahádúr Sháh was the last of the Balbaní dynasty; and the Emperor now appointed his own officers as Governors in

CHAP. III.] THE MUHAMMADAN RULE IN BENGAL. 21

Dehli, always spoke of Ghiyás-ud-dín with the greatest respect, and said that he well deserved the title of *Sultán* and the epithet *Supporter of the Faith.* The latter, however, unfortunately for himself, asserted his independence of the Dehli monarch; and having been reduced to submission and deprived of the Government of Bihár, again rebelled as soon as the troops of Altamsh had gone back to Dehli. Altamsh now sent an army into Bengal under his second son Násir-ud-dín, who defeated and slew the rebel, and became Governor of the province for the Emperor his father, A.D. 1227.

§ 6. *Tughán Khán* and *Tughral Khán.*—Prince Násir-ud-dín of Delhi reigned for some years in Bengal, and died at Lakhnautí during the lifetime of his father. He was nominally succeeded by an infant-brother, who received the same name, and afterwards became the Emperor Násir-ud-dín of Dehli. Three of Altamsh's generals were then Governors in succession; the third being *Tughán Khán*, who came to the throne in 1234, and reigned until 1245.

The reign of Tughán Khán is chiefly famous for the great war with the Rájá of Jájpur in Orissa. Tughán, having reduced the Rájá of Tirhut to submission, was about to invade Orissa, when he was met on the frontiers by the Rájá of Jájpur, and utterly routed. The Orissa army now invaded Bengal, took and plundered Nágor the capital of Bírbhúm, and laid siege to Lakhnautí. Tughán Khán in his distress applied to the Emperor of Dehli for assistance; and the Governor of Oudh, Timur Khán, marched into Bengal to his aid. The approach of Timur Khán forced the Jájpur troops to retire to Orissa; but Timur now determined to have Bengal for himself, and Tughán Khán after a severe battle was forced to resign the government to him. Tughán retired to Oudh, of which he was appointed Governor by the Emperor of Dehli. He had originally been a slave of the Emperor Altamsh; as also were the three next Governors of Bengal.

After two reigns of no importance, one of Tughán's successors, named *Tughral Khán*, endeavoured to take vengeance on the king of Orissa for this invasion of Bengal. Tughral Khán, who became Governor in A. D. 1253, marched into Orissa, and was at first successful; but in the third battle he was totally defeated and driven back to Bengal with ignominy. Similar reverses of fortune attended his invasion of Kámrúp; for having at first defeated the Rájá and plundered his capital, he was ultimately defeated, taken prisoner, and put to death, A.D. 1258.

§ 7. *Sultán Mughís-ud-dín Tughral.*—Three Governors of no great note intervened between the Tughral Khán, just spoken of, and his more famous namesake Tughral, who usurped the imperial title as *Sultán Mughís-ud-dín Tughral.* This active and daring officer obtained the government of Bengal by the favour of the Emperor Balban of Dehli; but having obtained immense wealth, many elephants, and much glory from a successful invasion of Tiparah, and hearing that Balban had grown old and weak, he assumed all the insignia of royalty as an independent monarch, pretending that Balban was dead. The Emperor, enraged at this ingratitude, immediately ordered the Governor of Oudh to march into Bengal; but Tughral utterly defeated this army, and also another stronger one that was subsequently sent against him. At last Balban, though now an old man, determined to march against the rebel in person; and Tughral, on his approach, fled towards Tiparah. The Emperor pursued; and after some time a detachment of his troops, that had been sent on ahead to get some news of the fugitive, obtained information of his whereabouts from some grain-merchants who had just supplied the rebel camp with food. It was a captain of the imperial army named Muhammad Sher who discovered this; and though he had only forty horsemen with him, he determined to attempt to seize Tughral. At headlong speed they rode into the rebel camp, shouting "Victory to the Great Sultán Balban." Tughral and his adherents fancied that the whole imperial army was upon them, and ran away in all directions. Tughral himself jumped on a horse without a saddle, and galloped towards the river; but he was seen and pursued by Malik, the brother of the captain Muhammad. Malik overtook him whilst his horse was swimming the river, and shot him with an arrow. Tughral fell from his

Lakhnautí, Sátganw, and Sunárganw. These however did not remain long undisturbed; and after much anarchy, the weakness of the Tughlaq Emperors led to the establishment of an independent line of kings in Bengal.

CHAPTER IV.

THE MUHAMMADAN RULE IN BENGAL. PART II.—THE INDEPENDENT KINGS OF BENGAL.

§ 1. Establishment of the Independence of Bengal. § 2. Ilyás Sháh. § 3. Sikandar Sháh. § 4. Sultán Ghiyás-ud-dín. § 5. The Hindú dynasty of Rájá Káns. § 6. The Ilyás Sháhí dynasty restored. § 7. The Habshí or Abyssinian Kings. § 8. The Husainí dynasty; Sultán Alá-ud-dín Husain Sháh. § 9. The Husainí dynasty continued. § 10. Review of the condition of the people during this period.

§ 1. *Establishment of the independence of Bengal.*—The most powerful of Muhammad bin Tughlaq's governors was Bahrám Khán of Sunárganw; and when he died in 1338, his armour-bearer Fakr-ud-dín Mubárak Sháh proclaimed himself independent king of Bengal. Shortly afterwards Alá-ud-dín Alí Sháh set up as independent king of Western Bengal. A legend says of Alí Sháh that a famous Muhammadan saint had appeared to him before he became king, and promised him the kingdom of Bengal on condition that he built a vault for the saint at Panduah (sometimes called Purruah) a place near Lakhnautí. Hence Alí Sháh chose this place as his capital. Great anarchy prevailed; Mubárak Sháh was defeated and killed by Alí Sháh; and Alí Sháh in his turn by Shams-ud-dín Ilyás Sháh, commonly called Hájí Ilyás, whose mother had been Alí Sháh's nurse.

§ 2. *Ilyás Sháh.*—Hájí Ilyás became master of Fírúzábad or Panduah in the year 1345; and in 1352 he established himself at Sunárganw also—thus uniting East and West Bengal, and founding a dynasty which lasted (with one short interruption) for nearly 150 years. This dynasty is sometimes called the Ilyás Sháhí dynasty.

As soon as Ilyás Sháh had secured his power in Bengal, he endeavoured to extend his dominions in the north-west, and marched as far as the Banáras district. To punish him for this encroachment, the emperor Firúz Sháh III., one of the weakest of the Tughlaq dynasty, raised a large army and marched with great pomp and magnificence into Bengal. Firúz took the capital Panduah, at the same time making prisoner the son of Ilyás. The latter threw himself into the strong fortress of Ekdálah, where he was besieged by the Emperor.

A story that is told about this siege, illustrates the boldness of Ilyás Sháh, and the resolution and courage which doubtless enabled him to establish his dynasty in Bengal. A celebrated saint named Rájá Bhaváni, much revered by Ilyás, happened to die near Ekdálah whilst Ilyás was shut up in the fortress. The latter was determined to attend the funeral; and disguising himself as a fakír, left the fortress, attended the funeral, and afterwards rode into the camp of the Emperor. The latter of course did not know him; so he was permitted to offer his respects as a fakír to Firúz, and then to depart unharmed. He returned safely to the besieged fortress; and the Emperor, when he heard of the exploit, though he was much vexed at having lost such an opportunity of seizing the rebel, could not but admire his bravery.

At last the emperor was obliged to give up the siege of Ekdálah and to acknowledge the independence of Bengal; and as Hájí Ilyás subsequently founded Hájípur opposite to Patná, he appears to have been confirmed in the possession of North Bihár as far as the Ghandak. This was A.D. 1353. Ilyás Sháh died in 1358.

§ 3. *Sikandar Sháh.*—The Emperor Firúz repeated his attempt to conquer Bengal as soon as he heard of the death of Ilyás; but the eldest son of the latter, who had succeeded with the title of *Sikandar Sháh*, successfully defended the fortress Ekdálah. Firúz returned to Dehli, taking with him some elephants and other presents which Sikandar gave him, A.D. 1359; and meddled no more in the affairs of Bengal. Sikandar has always been famous as the builder of the grand Adínah Masjid, of which the ruins are still to be seen at Panduah near Máldah. He was at length killed in a battle with his favourite son Ghiyás-ud-dín, who had been driven into rebellion by the wickedness of a jealous step-mother.

§ 4. *Sultán Ghiyás-ud-dín.*—The first act of the new Sultán was a very cruel one, though it has often been considered by Indian monarchs merely as a necessary act of self-preservation. This was the blinding of all his half-brothers, the sons of the jealous step-mother who had caused the quarrel between him and his father. But after this one wicked act, Ghiyás-ud-dín appears to have ruled with great justice and moderation; and an interesting story is told of his respect for the laws. Once upon a time, a poor widow brought an action against the king himself because he had accidentally wounded her son with an arrow whilst he was practising archery. The Kázi was almost afraid to summon the king before his court; but he thought it better to offend the king than to offend God, so at last he summoned him. The king came to the court, carrying a short sword under his garments. When at length the Kázi decided the case justly, and compelled the king to make full restitution, the king returned thanks to God that he had such an upright and fearless judge; and, drawing his sword and showing it to the Kázi, he said— "With this sword I would have cut off your head if you had judged unjustly." The Kázi, taking up the scourge wherewith condemned criminals were whipt, answered—"I also, for my part, swear that if you had not immediately obeyed the law, this whip should have made deep cuts in your back!" The king was much pleased, and handsomely rewarded the upright judge.

Ghiyás-ud-dín invited Háfiz, the famous poet of Shiráz in Persia, to come and live in Bengal; but Háfiz declined the invitation, as he feared to undertake such a long journey.

Some accounts say that Ghiyás-ud-din was killed by a powerful Hindú zamíndár, the Rájá of Bhatúriah and Dinájpur, called *Ganes* (he was called *Rájá Káns* by the Muhammadans). However this may be, it is certain that during the reigns of the son and grandson of Ghiyás-ud-dín, Rájá Ganes became very powerful; and at last succeeded in killing the grandson, and seating himself on the throne.

§ 5. *The Hindú dynasty of Rájá Káns.*—This dynasty, under Rájá Káns or Ganes, and his son and grandson, lasted for forty years from A.D. 1385 to 1425; but it was only Hindú for seven years, during the reign of Ganes himself, for his son became a Muhammadan. Ganes ruled with great impartiality, and was beloved equally by Musalmáns and Hindús. But during these reigns, the power of Bengal became less and its territories smaller; for the king of Assam conquered all the north-east of Bengal as far as the Karatayá river—and there were also successful invasions made by the Rájás of Tiparah, and by Ibráhim the great Sultán of Jaunpur.

[NOTE.—Owing to the weakness of the later kings of the Tughlaq dynasty at Dehli, many other provinces of the Dehli Empire had become independent like Bengal. One of the greatest of these was Jaunpur, whose capital was the city of Jaunpur in the province of Banáras. Here a Vazír of the Emperor Muhammad Tughlaq, named Kwájah Jahán, in 1393 founded an independent dynasty called the Sharkí dynasty. The greatest prince of this dynasty, Ibráhim Sháh Sharkí, came to the throne in 1401; in his reign the kingdom became very powerful, and he encroached much on the western frontier of Bengal, so as to include all Bihár in the empire of Jaunpur.]

Jatmall, the son of Rájá Ganes, became a Muhammadan under the name of Jalál-ud-dín Muhammad Sháh. During his reign, both Panduah and Gaur (so Lakhnautí is now again called) were beautified by magnificent buildings; and Gaur once more became the royal capital. His son Ahmad Sháh succeeded him in the year 1409. During his time, Ibráhim of Jaunpur invaded Bengal and took away many captives; these however he was compelled to release, by the threats of Sháh Rukh, the great Sultán of the Mughuls, who was then living in Persia, and was nominally Sultán of Hindústán as the successor of the great Sultán Timúr who had conquered Dehli in A.D. 1398. Ahmad was the last of the dynasty of Rájá Ganes; he oppressed his subjects very much, and at last was assassinated by two of his slaves, A.D. 1426.

§ 6. *The Ilyás Sháhí dynasty restored.*—After the assassination of Ahmad Sháh, a descendant of Ilyás Sháh, named Násir-ud-dín or *Násir Sháh*, was gladly set up by the adherents of the old Muhammadan dynasty. During his reign, the Kings of Jaunpur and Dehli were continually fighting with each other, so that the Jaunpur monarch was unable to interfere with Bengal; and in this way Násir Sháh reigned prosperously for thirty-two years, and strongly fortified the city of Gaur. He died in 1458; and between this time and the year 1483, the son, grandson, and great-grandson of Násir reigned in succession; the last being set aside after a few days by *Fath Sháh*, who appears to have been a younger son of Násir, and must consequently have been an old man at the time of his accession. He was assassinated at the instigation of the Abyssinian eunuch Bárbak, who became the first of the Habshí or Abyssinian kings of Bengal.

§ 7. *The Habshí Kings.*—During the reign of Bárbak Sháh, who was the son and successor of Násir Sháh, a large number of Abyssinian slaves and eunuchs had been introduced into Bengal for the protection of the kingdom and especially of the royal palace. These gradually became powerful and insolent; and after the assassination of Fath Sháh, one of them, named Bárbak (he was the eunuch who had contrived the murder), became king of Bengal under the curious title of *Sultán Sháhzádah*. He was himself in turn shortly afterwards killed by the Abyssinian commander-in-chief named Malik Indil Habshí, who assumed the title of *Sultán Firúz Sháh II*. He reigned with some success for three years, and was nominally succeeded by a descendant of the old Ilyás Sháhí dynasty named Mahmúd Sháh. The real ruler of the kingdom was an Abyssinian general named Habshí Khán; but both he and his master were soon assassinated by a cruel monster called Sídí Badr Diwánah, who frightfully oppressed the people for more than three years under the title of Muzaffar Sháh. At length the chiefs rebelled under the Vazír, Sayyid Alá-ud-dín Husain; Muzaffar was slain, and with him ended the dynasty of Habshí kings, A.D. 1489.

§ 8. *The Husainí Dynasty; Sultán Alá-ud-dín Husain Sháh.*— Sultán Alá-ud-dín Husain and his successor Nusrat Sháh were the two most powerful of all the independent kings of Bengal; their power was owing partly to the wars between Dehli and

Jaunpur and the weakness of the Dehli empire, but mainly to the ability and high character of Husain himself.

In the battle with Muzaffar Sháh outside the walls of Gaur, by which Husain Sháh obtained the throne, no less than 26,000 were slain. Husain then gave up the city of Gaur to be plundered by his soldiers; but finding that they carried the plundering to great excesses, and wantonly ill-treated the inhabitants, he caused twelve thousand of them to be put to death, and all their booty to be confiscated.

Husain Sháh had observed that much of the anarchy that had prevailed in Bengal during the troubled time of the Habshí kings, had been due to the turbulence of the mercenary soldiers (consisting partly of Abyssinians, and partly of native *Paiks* or "footguards") who had been employed nominally to protect the kingdom. So he now dismissed the Abyssinian troops altogether; and dispersed the *Paiks* by giving them small allotments of land on the frontiers of Orissa and in other troubled districts, on condition that they should defend the country against invasion.

[NOTE.—The Paiks, settled in the district of Midnapur on the frontiers of Orissa, gave much trouble to the English Government between the years 1790 and 1800 by their turbulent behaviour. *See* note, page 108.]

Husain Sháh invaded Assam, but made no permanent settlement there; he also attacked the powerful Rájá of Kámatápur (or Koch Bihár), near the slopes of the Himálaya mountains, took him prisoner, and destroyed the capital, which was a large town of nineteen miles in circumference. Husain left his son in charge of this territory; but the latter was driven out at a later period, and the Koch dynasty (to which belongs the present Rájá of Koch Bihár) established its power amongst these mountains in opposition to the kings of Bengal.

When the Emperor Sikandar Lodí of Dehli completed the conquest of the Jaunpur kingdom (which had been partially effected by his father Buhlol) by driving Husain Sháh, the last king of Jaunpur, out of his retreat in Bihár, the latter took refuge with his namesake in Bengal. The king of Bengal gave the fugitive king of Jaunpur an honourable asylum, and a pension; the latter lived happily at Gaur until his death, and the ruins of his magnificent tomb are still to be seen in that neighbourhood.

Husain Sháh seems, from some inscriptions that have been discovered, to have at one time possessed portions of Bihár, which had long belonged to Jaunpur; but in the year 1499, the Emperor Sikandar Lodí subdued that province, and threatened to invade Bengal. A treaty of peace however was concluded on the frontiers; the terms of which were (1) that the Emperor should retain his conquests in Bihár, provided he did not attempt to invade Bengal; and (2) that neither party should support or in any way assist the enemies of the other.

Sultán Alá-ud-dín after this enjoyed a happy and prosperous reign, beloved by his subjects, and respected by his neighbours. He ruled altogether twenty-four years; and though he died in 1520, more than three hundred and fifty years ago, his name is still remembered in Bengal from Orissa to the Brahmaputra as "Husain Sháh the Good."

§ 9. *The Husainí Dynasty continued.*—Husain Sháh was succeeded by his son Nusrat Sháh, who reaped all the advantages of his father's courage and wisdom. He at first seemed to deserve his good fortune; for he treated his brothers and other relations with great kindness, and at the same time displayed his military talents by conquering Tirhút, Hájípur, and Munger (*Monghyr*). He was enabled easily to effect these conquests, because Sultán Ibráhím Lodí and the Afgháns of Dehli were at this time hard pressed by Bábar, the great Mughul invader; and it has lately been proved that Nusrat for a short time occupied even a part of the North-Western Provinces. But at last Bábar and his Mughuls utterly defeated the Afgháns at the battle of Pánipat in 1526, and the empire of Dehli was transferred from the Afgháns to the Mughuls; and as many of the Afghán chiefs (including Mahmúd Lodí, brother of the late Sultán Ibráhím) obtained protection in Bengal from Nusrat Sháh, and as the latter had married the daughter of the late Sultán, Bábar determined to conquer Bengal. Twice however the king of Bengal succeeded in buying off the hostility of Bábar by very costly presents; and at length in 1529, the two monarchs concluded a solemn treaty of peace and amity. Nusrat however broke his word; for after the death of Bábar he again gave all the assistance he could to the Afghán chiefs, especially to Mahmúd Lodí, and concluded a treaty with Sultán Bahádur Sháh of Gujarát, who was the most formidable enemy of Bábar's son Humáyún.

At length Nusrat, who had made himself very much disliked by all the people and especially by his own servants, on account of his cruelty, was assassinated (A.D. 1533) by the eunuchs of the palace, because he had threatened to punish one of them very severely for a trivial offence. He is often called Nasíb Sháh, because Nasíb Khán was his name as a prince during the lifetime of his father Husain Sháh.

Nusrat's son and successor, Fírúz Sháh III., was almost immediately set aside and murdered by his uncle, Nusrat's brother Mahmúd Sháh III., who may be regarded as the last of the independent kings of Bengal—though we shall see that a short-lived dynasty maintained its existence for some time against Akbar the greatest of the Mughul Emperors. Mahmúd was ultimately defeated and deposed by the great Sher Khán (of whom an account will be given below), and compelled to take refuge with the Mughul Emperor Humáyún. Whilst Humáyún was engaged in endeavouring to put down Sher Khán, Mahmúd died of grief caused by his many misfortunes, and especially by the deaths of his two sons, who had fallen into the hands of Sher Khán's adherents, A.D. 1538-39.

§ 10. *Review of the condition of the People under the Afghán Kings.*—The magnificent architecture which was characteristic of the period treated of in this chapter, of which we see the remains in the ruins at Gaur, Panduah, and elsewhere, shows that the people of Bengal had arrived at a high pitch of civilisation in some points of art; and that the higher classes, or at least the king and his courtiers, lived in a state of considerable comfort and often of luxury. But the money expended on these great works was wrung from the poor, who were always oppressed; and the incessant wars that disturbed the land often prevented the peasants from tilling the soil, and thus increased their sufferings. In these wars, not the slightest care was taken of life or property, as is evident in the sacking of the great and rich city of Gaur by the soldiers of a man who nevertheless was called "the good"—*viz.*, Husain Sháh. In the account of that event, it is stated that the rich inhabitants of Gaur were in the habit of using gold dishes for their food; and that a man's respectability was judged by the number of gold dishes he could display at banquets. This shows that a great deal of luxury was prevalent. It is also stated that Husain Sháh, though a good and kind man generally, thought it no harm to give up Gaur to be sacked by his soldiers, because most of the people were Hindús and not Muhammadans. At the same time, the many fine tanks and saráis that were built by these kings of Gaur, prove that they were not entirely selfish, and that they were willing to help their subjects sometimes.

CHAPTER V.

THE MUHAMMADAN RULE IN BENGAL. PART III.—THE DYNASTY OF SHER SHAH.

§ 1. Sher Sháh Sur. § 2. Sher's successors of the Sur family. § 3. Sulaimán Kararáni. § 4. Dáúd Khán, the last of the Afghán kings of Bengal.

§ 1. *Sher Sháh Sur.*—Sher Sháh was an Afghán belonging to the Sur family or tribe. He was at first a *jágírdár* (*i.e.*, one who holds land from the king on condition of serving him in the wars) of Sahsarám in West Behár. He had greatly distinguished himself as a youth by his courage and prudence; and once on a time, while hunting with Sultán Mahmúd Loháni, had killed an enormous tiger with one blow of his sword—for which exploit he was given the title of Sher Khán (his name had originally been *Faríd*).

In 1528, Sher Khán made his submission to Bábar, whom he accompanied on a great expedition against a place called Chánderi, the last stronghold of the Rájpúts who had opposed the Mughul invasion. An anecdote is related of Sher Khán's conduct during this campaign, that well illustrates his character. He was once dining at the Emperor's own table, and some food was set before him which could not be eaten without being first cut with a knife. Now the servants had been ordered not to give him a knife, because he was considered to be a man of too dangerous a character to be trusted with a knife in the emperor's presence. Sher called for a knife; and when he was not immediately supplied, he drew his dagger, cut the food with it, and made a hearty meal without caring for the jeers of the courtiers who were astonished at this unceremonious conduct. Bábar, who had been remarking his behaviour, turned to one of his friends and said—"This Afghán will one day be a great man, for he is not turned from his purpose by trifling difficulties."

Sher Khán on his return became Vazír of Jalál-ud-dín Loháni, who was for a short time the Afghán King of Bihár; and ultimately acquired the sole power in the province, as the king fled to Bengal, being afraid of Sher's increasing power. In the following year, 1529, Mahmúd Lodí made himself master of Bihár; but Bábar, returning with his army, drove him away into Bengal, and putting in an officer of his own as Governor, left Sher Khán in possession of his paternal jágírs.

In 1531, Sher Khán obtained possession of the strong fortress of Chunár in the province of Banáras, by a marriage with the widow of the Afghán officer who had held it since the breaking up of the Afghán empire of Dehli; and from this time his progress was rapid, though sometimes varied by reverses.

In 1536, he captured Gaur, notwithstanding the assistance which Mahmúd Sháh III. the king of Bengal [see Chap. IV., § 9] obtained from the Portuguese; and drove Mahmúd to take refuge with the Mughuls, who were now commanded by Humáyún the son of Bábar. About this time also, by a detestable act of treachery, Sher obtained possession of the impregnable fortress of Rahtás on the river Son in Bihár, which was of the greatest value to him as it afforded him a place of security wherein to place his family and the immense treasures which he had acquired by the capture of Gaur.

In the meantime Humáyún had overrun the greater portion of

Western Bengal, and now occupied Gaur. But Sher, retiring westward, seized Banáras and took possession of the passes into Bengal, thus cutting off Humáyún's retreat; whilst at the same time one of Humáyún's brothers proclaimed himself Emperor at Agra. Sher now assumed the title of Sháh, as king of Bengal and Bihár. Humáyún, after waiting several months at Gaur, was at length alarmed at the progress made by his enemies; and determined to try to make good his retreat to Dehli, A.D. 1539. The two armies met at Chausá or Chúparghát, at the confluence of the Karmanásá and the Ganges, between Patna and Banáras; and for nearly three months they lay encamped at a short distance apart, neither side daring to make the attack. At length Sher had recourse to the disgraceful means by which he had succeeded in taking Rahtás—viz., perfidy and fraud. He solemnly swore on the Korán that he would allow the Mughul army to pass in safety, on condition that Humáyún acknowledged him as King of Bengal and Bihár; and that very night, he made a sudden attack on the Mughuls, who were feasting in honour of the peace; he killed a large number, and the rest escaped with great difficulty. The Emperor himself had only time to leap on his horse and plunge into the Ganges; he would have been drowned in the stream, had he not been rescued by a water-carrier; and he reached Agra almost alone. Sher Sháh made the most of the advantage which he had thus treacherously obtained; for he employed the following year in consolidating his Government in Bengal, and in besieging Jaunpur; and then marched, at the head of 50,000 Afgháns, to expel Humáyún from India. In this attempt he was completely successful; for in the decisive battle of Kanauj, he utterly defeated Humáyún, and thus for a short time restored the Afgháns to the empire of Hindústán from which Bábar and his Mughuls had thrust them.

Sher Sháh, though still king of Bengal, was now Emperor of Dehli as well; and his history is not connected much further with that of Bengal, which enjoyed uninterrupted prosperity during his reign. He only once returned to this part of his empire, to put down an ambitious viceroy; at the same time he divided Bengal into provinces, over each one of which he placed a Governor. In 1545 he was killed by the bursting of a shell at the siege of Kálinjhar in Bandelkhand.

In his government, both of Bengal and of the Empire, Sher Sháh was wise, active, and benevolent; but all the excellence of his character, both public and private, was marred by a faithlessness which must disgust every one. The security and quiet of the country under his government was remarkable; insomuch that travellers and merchants, throwing down their goods, went to sleep at the side of the highway without fear of robbery. He made a splendid road from Sunárganw in Eastern Bengal, to the Indus, with a saráí or rest-house at each stage, wells at intervals of a mile and half, rows of fruit-trees on each side, and many masjids; and ordered that all travellers, without distinction of race or religion, should be entertained at each stage at the public expense. He also established, for the first time in India, a horse-post, for forwarding quick intelligence to the Government and for the advantage of trade and correspondence.

§ 2. *Sher's successors of the Sur family.*—Sher Sháh and his family reigned in Dehli as Emperors of Hindústán, from 1540 to 1556; but Sher's son, Islám Sháh, when he came to the imperial throne, neglected the prudent precautions of his father with regard to Bengal, and united the whole province under a chief related to himself, named *Muhammad Khán Sur*. The latter, however, was faithful to his benefactor Islám; but as soon as the infamous Muhammad Adil Sháh made himself master of Dehli, Muhammad Khán Sur declared his independence, and seized some districts beyond his own limits, in Jaunpur. In the following year, A.D. 1555, however, he was defeated and slain by Hemú, the famous commander-in-chief of Muhammad Adil's army.

Bahádur Sháh, the son and successor of Muhammad Khán, avenged his father's death by defeating and killing Muhammad Adil Sháh in the great battle of Munger (Mongbyr), A.D. 1556. He was succeeded by his brother Jalál-ud-dín, and the latter by his son, a youth who was slain by an obscure person who usurped the Government for a short time.

§ 3. *Sulaimán Kuraráni.*—The chief of the Kararáni tribe of

Afgháns, named Sulaimán Kararáni, had been appointed Governor of Bihár by Islám Sháh, son of Sher Sháh Sur, Emperor of Dehli. In the times of anarchy that followed the death of Islám Sháh, Sulaimán had declared his independence, and had aided Bahádur Sháh of Bengal at the battle of Munger. He now sent his brother Táj Khán into Bengal with a powerful army; the latter easily subdued the obscure usurper, and reigned at Gaur for a year as his brother's deputy. In the year 1564 Táj Khán died; Sulaimán then proceeded himself to Bengal, and made *Tándah* his capital—a place (now deserted) opposite Gaur on the right side of the Ganges.

The great Emperor Akbar, the greatest of all the Mughul Emperors, had now succeeded Humáyún in Dehli; and, with the aid of his famous General Bairám Khán, had thoroughly subdued the adherents of the Afghán dynasty of Sher Sháh Sur. Sulaimán, therefore, as soon as he had obtained possession of Bengal, sent an envoy to Akbar with valuable presents and promises of attachment. By this prudent behaviour, which he continued to maintain, Sulaimán secured the friendship of Akbar and the peace of Bengal throughout his reign, which lasted until A.D. 1573.

The only event of the reign which was very important, was the conquest of Orissa in 1567. Rájá Pratáp Chandra Deo, the last monarch of the Gangá Vansa dynasty, had died in 1532; and a period of anarchy had followed in Orissa. Rájá Mukund Deo was now king; and he was the last *Gajpati*, or "Lord of Elephants," as the native independent kings of Orissa were called. Sulaimán's first attempt to conquer Mukund Deo was unsuccessful; but he subsequently sent his famous General Kálápahár to complete the conquest, aided by the king's own son Báyazíd, who marched into Orissa over the mountains of Jhárkand (or Chutíá Nágpur). Kálápahár was originally a Bráhman; but he had become a Muhammadan in order to marry a beautiful princess of the royal family of Bengal, who had fallen in love with him. He had now become a ferocious persecutor of the Hindús, and especially of Bráhmans; his conquest of Orissa was marked by the greatest cruelty, and the Uriyás retained for centuries the remembrance of the atrocities perpetrated by him, and of the rage with which he destroyed every idol and pulled down every temple. He is especially famous for the sack of the great temple of Jagannáth at Púrí. He was wounded in the battle of Akmahall; and killed many years afterwards, in one of the fights between Qutlu Khán [*see* § 4, and Chap. VI., § 3] and the Mughul Generals.

The conquest of Orissa was disgraced by a base act of treachery. Sultán Ibráhím Súr, a nephew of Sher Sháh, who for a short time had been Emperor of Dehli, had established himself in Orissa after he had been driven out of Dehli. Sulaimán now invited him to a conference, and basely assassinated him. Sulaimán left Khán Jahán as Governor of Orissa; Qutlu Khán being the subordinate Governor of Púrí. He now attempted to effect the conquest of Koch Bihár; but was prevented by a rebellion which broke out in Orissa. This was successfully put down; and from this time, Sulaimán applied himself to the peaceful administration of his dominions.

- § 4. *Dáúd Khan, the last of the Afghán Kings of Bengal.*—Báyazíd, the son of Sulaimán, was soon set aside by the Afghán chiefs of Bengal, in favour of Dáúd Khán. Dáúd foolishly abandoned the conciliatory policy of Sulaimán towards the Emperor Akbar; and proclaimed his independence by ordering the *Khutba** to be read, and coin to be struck, in his own name. The prudence and good government of Sulaimán had accumulated an immense treasure; together with an army numbering 180,000 men, with 20,000 cannons and 3,600 elephants. Elated by the possession of these great resources, Dáúd determined to encroach on the Mughul dominions; and accordingly seized Zamániyá (now a station on the East Indian Railway), a fortress near Ghazípur, lately erected by one of Akbar's officers for a frontier garrison. Akbar quickly sent against him, into Bihár, Munim Khán, one of his best generals, who was now *Khánkhánán* (*i.e.*, commander-in-chief) and *Vakíl of the Empire*. Munim Khán made peace

---

* The *khutba* was the public prayer offered up in Muhammadan countries for the reigning sovereign; it could only be used for independent kings.

CHAP. V.]   THE MUHAMMADAN RULE IN BENGAL.   39

with Dáúd's Governor of Bihár on very easy terms; but both Akbar and Dáúd refused to be bound by this treaty; and Akbar actually sent one of his Hindú generals, the famous financier Rájá Todar Mall Khatrí, to supersede Munim Khán. The latter however marched back at once and besieged Dáúd in Patna, in the early part of the year 1574. As Patná held out, Munim induced Akbar to come himself to the seat of war with reinforcements. Akbar came by water with a fleet of boats, soon captured the town of Hájípur opposite to Patna, and sent the heads of the Governor and his chief officers to Dáúd. The latter was frightened, and fled in a swift boat by night to Tándah; Patna was taken by Akbar, and the fugitives pursued for fifty miles—after which Akbár returned to Agra, leaving Munim Khán as Governor of Bihár and Bengal, with orders to pursue Dáúd.

Dáúd had stopped, on his way to Tándah, at the famous pass of Teliágarhí near Rájmahall; and finding its fortifications very strong, strictly ordered its garrison to defend it to the last extremity. The garrison however, seeing that their king had himself fled to Tándah, and being warned by the fate of the garrison of Hájípur, ran away; so Munim Khán got possession of it without the loss of a single man. Dáúd, immediately on hearing of this mishap, fled to Orissa; and Munim occupied the capital of Bengal.

The Rájá Todar Mall was now sent after Dáúd into Orissa. But he was at first unsuccessful; and dissensions breaking out between him and his officers, Munim Khán was himself compelled to march from Tándah to his aid. Many skirmishes had already taken place; and the combined imperial forces at length came up with Dáúd and his army at a place between Midnapur and Jellasor *(Medinipur* and *Jaleswara)* called TAKAROI or MUGHULMARI. The battle of Mughulmárí is one of the most important in the annals of Bengal; it was fought on March 3, 1575. The numbers of troops on each side were about equal; but Dáúd's army excelled in elephants, which had been clothed with black yak tails and skins of wild beasts, so as to increase the terror of their appearance and frighten the horses of the Mughuls. Munim Khán had the advantage of a number of small cannons mounted on gun-carriages. The battle raged long with the greatest fury on both sides. Munim's cannon put to flight the elephants of Dáúd; but the Afghán cavalry charged the Mughuls with such valour and resolution, that Munim Khán himself was wounded and nearly captured, many of his bravest officers were killed, and the whole line of the Mughuls was thrown into confusion. The Hindú Rájá Todar Mall, however, retrieved the fortune of the day by his undaunted firmness. "What matters it," cried he, "if Khán Alam is dead? what fear, if the Khán Khánán has run away? the empire is ours!" So saying, he rallied the Mughul line which had already begun to waver; once more they charged the Afgháns; and the timid Dáúd, alarmed at the death of some of his favourite officers, fled hastily from the field. The battle of Mughulmárí was won; and with it, the supremacy in Bengal passed from the Afgháns to the Mughuls, notwithstanding several attempts of the former to recover their lost power.

Todar Mall pursued Dáúd to Katak (*Cuttack*); and near this place, Munim Khán having coming up in the meanwhile, Dáúd threw himself on the mercy of the emperor, gave up his sword to Munim, and was presented by the latter with the sovereignty of Katak as a vassal of the empire. Munim left Mughul Governors in the other portions of Orissa, and returned to Tándah.

Shortly afterwards Munim Khán very unwisely ordered the seat of Government to be transferred from Tándah to Gaur, though the season was very unsuitable for such a change, as it was in the middle of the rains. A dreadful pestilence broke out almost immediately; vast numbers of the people and soldiers, and even many grandees, died; and at length Munim Khán himself was carried off by it. From this time Gaur, the most ancient and formerly by far the greatest of all the cities of Bengal, was gradually deserted by its inhabitants. A few years later, at the time of the Great Military Rebellion in Bengal [*see* Chap. VI., § 2] we hear of the rebels seizing it as an important place; but very soon it sinks altogether out of notice, and for centuries its magnificent ruins have been buried in jungle, the haunt only of wild beasts.

Immediately on the death of Munim Khán, all the Afgháns

CHAP. VI.] THE MUHAMMADAN RULE IN BENGAL. 41

in Bengal and Orissa flew to arms; and Dáúd, unmindful of the oath of allegiance which he had sworn after the battle of Mughulmárí, marched through Bengal, expelling all the Mughul garrisons, and took up a strong position, guarded on one side by the mountains and on the other by the Ganges, at Akmahall (now called Rájmahall). The emperor, on hearing the news, appointed Husain Kulí Khán (who had received the title of *Khán Jahán*, which was only second in the Mughul army to that of Khán Khánán) as Munim's successor; Rájá Todar Mall being again appointed second in command. Khán Jahán repulsed the Afghán outposts at the pass of Teliágarhí; and then marched on to Akmahall, where he immediately commenced the siege of Dáúd's entrenchments. At length, one of Dáúd's best generals was killed in a skirmish; and this brought on a general battle— the battle of Akmahall, 1576.

In the battle Todar Mall again distinguished himself as before. The right wing of the Afghán army was under the command of the ferocious conqueror of Orissa, Kálá Pahár [see § 3]; and Dáúd himself led the centre. Whilst the fortune of the day was still undecided, Kálá Pahár was seen to fall wounded, and the Afgháns under his command immediately gave way. Khán Jahán, seeing his advantage, charged with the Mughul centre straight upon Dáúd's position; and the whole Afghán army turned and fled. Dáúd himself was captured, and brought before Khán Jahán, who sent his head to the emperor Akbar at Agra.

CHAPTER VI.

THE MUHAMMADAN RULE IN BENGAL. PART IV.—THE MUGHUL SUBAHDARS UNDER THE EMPERORS OF DEHLI.

§ 1. Khán Jahán, and the Settlement of Bengal. § 2. The Great Military Revolt of the Mughul Jágírdárs of Bengal. § 3. The First Afghán Rebellion. § 4. Rájá Mán Singh, and the Subjugation of the Afgháns. § 5. The Story of Sher Afkan. § 6. The Collection of the Revenue. § 7. The Final Subjugation of the Afgháns in Bengal. § 8. Review of the Condition of the People. § 9. The Portuguese Wars in Bengal. § 10. Ibráhím Khán, and the Rebellion of Sháh Jahán. § 11. Islám Khán Mashhadí. § 12. Settlement of the English in Bengal. § 13. Condition of the People under Sultán Shujá. § 14. Shujá's Attempt on the Empire. § 15. Mír Júmlah. § 16. Sháistah Khán. § 17. Sháistah Khán's Quarrel with the English Merchants. § 18. The Nawáb Ibráhím Khán; the Rebellion of Sobhá Singh, and the fortification of Calcutta by the English. § 19. Sultán Azim-us-Shán; the English allowed to purchase the Zamíndárí of Calcutta. § 20. The Union of the Old and New East India Companies. § 21. The Rise of Murshid Kulí Khán. § 22. Murshid Kulí Khán as Governor of Bengal. § 23. Surgeon Hamilton, and the English Embassy to Dehli. § 24. Nawáb Shujá-ud-dín. § 25. The Rise of Alí Virdí Kháu. § 26. Shujá-ud-dín *continued*, and his son Sarfaráz Khán.

§ 1. *Khán Jahán and the Settlement of Bengal.*—After the decisive battle of Akmahall, Khán Jahán sent Rájá Todar Mall back to Akbar, with all the booty he had obtained, and the elephants of the Afgháns. He himself pursued the remains of Dáúd's army, came up with them at Sátganw,* and utterly dispersed them. He employed the next two years in suppressing the Afghán power in various parts of these provinces, and in reducing the Rájá of Koch Bihár to submission; and before his death, which occurred near Tándah in 1578, nearly the whole of Bengal, Bihár and Orissa had submitted to him.

§ 2. *The Great Military Revolt of the Mughul Jágírdárs of Bengal.*—Muzaffar Khán, who had been Diwán of the Empire, was appointed by the Emperor Akbar to succeed Khán Jahán.

When Munim Khán first conquered Bengal [*see* Chapter V., § 4], he sent one of his officers, named Majnún Khán Qáqshál, the chief of the Qáqshál tribe of Afgháns, to Ghorághát, with orders to put down the Afgháns of Northern Bengal. Majnún

---

* Sátganw, near Hugli, was at this time a port of great importance, at which much of the royal customs-duties were levied on goods exported and imported. Formerly a large branch of the Ganges flowed by Sátganw to Tamluk; but this river dried up long ago, and consequently the trade of Sátganw died out. At present the place is an insignificant village of a few huts. In Muhammadan times, it had the nickname of *Bulghák khánah* or place of rebellion.

CHAP. VI.] THE MUHAMMADAN RULE IN BENGAL. 43

was successful; and, settling himself in the district as if he were a Jágírdár appointed by the Emperor, he collected around him the whole Qáqshál tribe, and divided the land amongst them, only requiring from them their personal service as soldiers in case he should need it.

[NOTE.—A *Jágírdár* is the holder of a *jágír*,—*i.e.*, land given (generally as a reward for distinguished conduct) to a person on condition of his performing certain services to the supreme lord. These services were nearly always of a military nature,—*i.e.*, the Jágírdár was bound to attend his lord in time of need with a specified number of troops; and if the rules were exactly followed, the surplus revenues of the jágír, after paying the stipends of the Jágírdár himself and his troops, ought to be paid to the supreme lord.

The plan which Majnún introduced into Bengal, of allowing his officers to hold subordinate *Jágírs* under him, had long been in use amongst the Afgháns. The whole system is very much like that which was long prevalent amongst the warlike nations of Europe under the name of the FEUDAL SYSTEM.]

Many other great Mughul officers had followed the example of Majnún Khán; and consequently a great deal of the land of Bengal, Bihár, and Orissa was now held by these powerful Military Jágírdárs, who paid very little revenue to the Emperor. About this time, Sháh Mansúr, the Imperial Vazír, was introducing many reforms into the management of the revenues of the empire; and Muzaffar Khán, at the instigation of Sháh Mansúr, determined to make these Jágírdárs account strictly for the revenues of their jágírs, and to prevent any one of them remaining too long in one jágír so as to obtain permanent possession of it. But as soon as he commenced to carry out Sháh Mansúr's orders, many of the chief Jágírdárs broke out into open rebellion. Of these the greatest were Masúm Khán Kábulí, a most distinguished officer who had been wounded in a fight with Kálá Pahár, and Bábá Khán, the young chief of the Qáqshál Afgháns of Ghorághát.

Muzaffar Khán defeated the Bengal rebels several times; but at length the Jágírdárs of Bihár under Masúm Khán Kábulí forced the Pass of Teliágarhí, joined the Qáqsháls and others in Bengal, and laid siege to Táudah. The rebels at first would have submitted if they could have obtained the Emperor's pardon and permission to settle on new jágírs in Orissa; but Muzaffar foolishly showed them his weakness by shutting himself up in the fort of Tándah, which was little better than four mud walls—and now the rebels demanded the most exorbitant terms. They proceeded to storm the fortress, captured Muzaffar and put him to death; and thus were for a time masters of the province.

The Emperor Akbar at this crisis sent the Rájá Todar Mall as Governor of Bengal and Bihár. At first, by his influence with the Hindú Zamíndárs, the Rájá succeeded in preventing the rebels from getting any supplies of food; and in this way, he drove them to retire into Bengal (some even took refuge with Isá, the great zamíndár of Orissa), and brought the whole of Bihár again under the imperial sway. But there was much jealousy between the Hindú Rájá and the Muhammadan Generals who were his colleagues; and Akbar was at length obliged to recall Todar Mall, and appoint the great general Aziz to his place with the title of Khán Azam.

[NOTE.—Todar Mall after this was appointed Vakíl of the Mughul Empire; and in that capacity he carried out the finaucial reforms for which he is so famous. He drew up a new Rent-roll for the whole empire; in which the land-revenue of Bengal was assessed in 1582 at about one crore and seven lakhs of rupees. This was levied from the ryots in money, as the equivalent of the *fourth share* of the entire produce of the land claimed by the sovereign as proprietary lord of the soil. The great historian of this period, Abul Fazl, says of the revenue of Bengal, "The ryots of Bengal are obedient and ready to pay the taxes. During eight months of the year they pay the required sums by instalments. They personally bring the money in rupees and gold muhurs to the appointed place. Payment in kind is not usual. The amount of the land-tax is settled by the Collector and the ryot."

Todar Mall also ordered that all Government accounts should be kept in Persian, instead of in Hindí as formerly; it was in consequence of this that the Hindús first began to cultivate Persian, and in this way a new dialect called *Urdu* (compounded of Persian and Hindí) arose in Upper India. Like Rájá Mán Singh and many other Hindús in Akbar's time, Todar Mall was one of the chief grandees of the Mughul Court, and was a Commander of 4,0C0.]

The Khán Azam, by sowing dissensions amongst the hostile Jágírdárs, continued to detach them one by one from the rebel cause; so that before the end of the year 1582, he took quiet possession of the capital Tándah, and this rebellion (one of the most dangerous that ever threatened the stability of the Mughul Empire) was at an end.

§ 3. *The First Afghán Rebellion.*—During the time that the Emperor's officers in Bengal had been hard-pressed by the Great Military Revolt, the Afgháns, who had been so recently conquered, again collected together under Qutlu Khán [*see* Chap. V., § 3], recovered the whole of Orissa, and much of Western Bengal as far as the river Damúdar. In 1583, a treaty had been arranged between an officer of Khán Azam and Qutlu Khán; but it was broken off owing to the arrogance of some of the Afgháns. Qutlu Khán was compelled to take refuge in the forests, but as Khán Azam at this time left the province of Bengal and returned to Agra, the Mughul successes were not followed up; and Khán Azam's successor, Sháhbáz Khán, who was only Súbahdár for a few months, gave up to the Afgháns the whole of Orissa, on condition that they should not interfere with any part of Bengal.

§ 4. *Rájá Mán Singh, and the Subjugation of the Afgháns.*[*]— Sháhbáz Khán was recalled, because it was believed that he had been bribed to give the Afgháns such easy terms. Another Governor was appointed, who, however, very soon died; and then at last, in 1587, Akbar appointed Rájá Mán Singh of Amber or Jaipur—perhaps the greatest of all the great men who at this time adorned the Mughul Court, and a general and statesman of whom the Hindús are to this day justly proud.

Kumár Mán Singh (he did not become Rájá until the death of his father in 1590) was the son of Rájá Bhagaván Dás, and the grandson of Rájá Bihári Mall; a chief of the Kachwáwah

---

[*] An interesting Bengáli romance, called *Durgeshanandini*, by Bábu Bankim Chandra Chattopádhyáya, is founded on the events narrated in this and the preceding sections.

Rájpúts, and 20th in descent from the founder of Amber (the present Mahárájá of Jaipur is 34th in descent). His sister was married to Prince Salím (afterwards the Emperor Jahángír); of which marriage Prince Khusrau was the offspring. Mán Singh had already served with the highest distinction in the Panjáb and elsewhere, and was a commander of 5,000.

His first attempts to conquer Orissa were unsuccessful, mainly owing to the disobedience of his deputy-governor, who neglected to bring the necessary reinforcements. Indeed his son Jagat Singh was actually taken prisoner by the Afghans, who were highly elated at their victory; but fortunately for the Rájá, Qutlu Khán died a few days after, and the Afghán chiefs sent back their prisoner Jagat Singh with proposals for peace. Rájá Mán Singh was very glad of this, for the rains had set in, and he was unable to march against the rebels; so he made an agreement with the great zamíndár Isá, who was the guardian of Qutlu Khán's children, that the Afgháns should retain Orissa, on condition of their putting the Emperor's name on all coins and public edicts, and of their giving up to himself the sacred temple of Jagannáth at Púrí.

This treaty was faithfully observed during the life of Isá; but after his death two years later, the other Afghán chiefs, under Usmán, the son of Isá Khán, seized and plundered the rich lands of the temple of Jagannáth. At this the Rájá, as a Hindú, was much incensed; he invaded Orissa with all his forces, and in a great battle on the banks of the river Súbanrekha totally defeated the Afghán army, and once more annexed Orissa to the Mughul Empire. He sent no less than 120 elephants taken from the Afgháus to the Emperor at Agra; and then took up his residence at Akmahall, which he now made the capital of Bengal, under the name of Rájmahall. He built there a palace and strong fortifications; and ultimately the city increased so much in size and fame, that the Muhammadans called it Akbarnagar in honour of the Emperor.

In 1595, Rájá Mán Singh married the sister of Lakshmí Náráyana, the Rájá of Koch Bihár, who had declared himself a vassal of the Mughul Empire. Lakshmí Náráyana was in consequence of this set aside by his relations and subjects; but Mán Singh soon sent an army into Koch Bihár and restored him. This was the first time that the Mughuls obtained a footing in that part of Bengal.

In the year 1598, Mán Singh, at the command of the Emperor, left Bengal to join the Mughul army in the Dakhin, his son Jagat Singh remaining behind as deputy. The latter however soon died; and the Afgháns of Orissa seized the opportunity once more to rebel. Under the command of Usmán Khán they met the imperial army near Bhadrak in Balasor, and completely routed it, and then made themselves masters of a great portion of Bengal. On hearing this, Rájá Mán Singh, who was at Ajmír, hastened into Bengal; he halted at the strong fortress of Rahtás to collect all his followers, and then marched against the Afgháns. He met them at *Sherpur Atái*, a place between Bardwán and Murshidábád, and totally routed them, compelling Usmán Khán to fly to Orissa. After this victory, the Rájá paid a short visit to the Emperor; when he was promoted to be a commander of seven thousand, being thus raised to a rank higher than that of any other subject.

He continued to govern Bengal with great wisdom and justice until the year 1604; when a report that the Emperor Akbar was likely to die, caused him to resign his governorship and return to Agra. He did this because he was anxious that his sister's son Prince Khusrau, instead of her husband Prince Salím, should succeed Akbar as Emperor. He was unable to effect this purpose; and Salím succeeded in 1605 under the title of the Emperor Jahángír. Jahángír thought it prudent to forgive Mán Singh for having opposed him; so he reappointed him Governor of Bengal—but in a few months he recalled him to make way for his own foster-brother Shaikh Khúbú, on whom he had bestowed the title of Kutb-ud-dín Khán.

[NOTE.—Rájá Mán Singh after this enjoyed a life of ease for some years in Rájpútána, where he raised levies to aid Jahángír in the Dakhin. He at last marched to the Dakhin, where he died in 1615. It is related that sixty of his fifteen hundred wives burned themselves on his funeral

pile; only one of his numerous sons was alive at the time of his death—
Rájá Bhao Singh, who succeeded to his title and estates.]

§ 5. *The Story of Sher Afkan.*—The Emperor Jahángír, during the life of his father Akbar, had fallen in love with a very beautiful woman named Mihrunnisá, and wished to marry her; but Akbar disapproved of the marriage, and by his wish the lady was married to a young Persian of noble family named *Sher Afkan*, who was made Governor (*tuyúldár*) of Bardwán. Jahángír however still wickedly hoped to be able to marry Mihrunnisá, either by inducing her husband to divorce her, or by killing Sher Afkan. Accordingly, as soon as he became Emperor, he appointed his foster-brother *Kutb-ud-dín Khán* (in 1606) to be Governor of Bengal, because he could be sure of his aid in the matter; and then he ordered him to send Sher Afkan to Court, but the latter refused to go. Kutb then went to Bardwán, having first sent on his nephew to assure Sher that no harm would be done to him. When Kutb arrived, Sher Afkan went to meet him, accompanied by two men. On his approach, Kutb lifted up his horsewhip as a sign for his men to cut down Sher Afkan. "What is all this?"—exclaimed Sher. Kutb then waved his hand to call back his men; and advancing towards Sher, upbraided him for his disobedience. Kutb's men, mistaking his signal, began to close around Sher; who immediately rushed on the Súbahdár and gave him a deep wound with his sword in the abdomen. Some of the nobles surrounding Kutb attempted to cut down the lion-like Sher—but they too fell a sacrifice to his terrible sword; till at length, large numbers pressing round him, he was borne to the ground covered with a multitude of wounds. Kutb was still on horseback, when he was told that Sher Afkan had been killed; and he gave the necessary orders about the disposal of Sher's family and property. But his wound was a mortal one, for his bowels were protruding through it, though he had supported them with his hand; he died as he was being carried away in a palanquin.

[NOTE.—Mihrunnisá bore the death of her husband with great fortitude, and after a time became the famous empress Núr Jahán. Jahángír, in his book called the *Tuzuk*, expresses the most ungenerous pleasure at the death

CHAP. VI.] THE MUHAMMADAN RULE IN BENGAL. 49

of Sher Afkan, adding his hope that "the black-faced wretch will for ever remain in hell."]

§ 6. *The Collection of the Revenues.*—Kutb-ud-dín's successor in the Súbah of Bengal was *Jahángír Kulí Khán*, who conquered and slew the famous Sankara Ráma, Rájá of Gorákhpur, in 1607. He was however chiefly known for the cruel rigour with which he personally exacted the revenues. He was always accompanied by a hundred trumpeters who, whenever any one disputed any point of revenue with him, made such a dreadful noise as to terrify the defaulters into submission; and in case this failed, he had also with him a hundred Kashmírian archers who could bring down the smallest bird in its flight, and whose arrows were ready to be lodged in the breast of any one pointed out to them.

§ 7. *The Final Subjugation of the Afgháns in Bengal.*— Shaikh Islám Khán succeeded Jahángír Kulí; and under his rule occurred the last attempt of the Orissa Afgháns to recover their lost power in Bengal. Usmán was probably the son of Isá Khán, the chief of the Loháni Afgháns, though he has generally been called the son of Qutlu Khán [*see* § 4]; he was now the acknowledged head of the Afgháns, and determined to assert his independence. But Islám Khán sent against him a brave and experienced officer named Shujáat Khán. The fight took place somewhere in Eastern Bengal. Usmán Khán having caused his elephant to be driven against Shujáat, the latter wounded the elephant with his own spear; and Usmán was finally struck in the forehead by a bullet, and expired during the night. After this decisive defeat, the relations of Usmán submitted to the Emperor, and his brother became one of Jahángír's courtiers. Shujáat Khán received from the emperor the title of *Rustam-i-zamán* (the Hercules of the Age) as a reward for his bravery; and Islám Khán was also promoted.

§ 8. *Review of the condition of the People.*—Thus in 1612 expired the last remains of Afghán power in Bengal. For more than 370 years, from the conquest of Nadiyá by Bakhtyár Khiljí in 1203, to the battle of Akmahall in 1576, they had been the rulers of these great provinces; and for a further term of 36 years their turbulence and dislike to the Mughul rule had kept

the country in a continual state of disorder, and had frequently devastated it with fire and sword and all the horrors of war. During the whole of this time, the native Hindús, who formed the bulk of the population, were utterly neglected, where they were not maltreated; in times of peace they were allowed to cultivate the land and carry on commerce, in order that the wealth thus produced might yield a rich harvest of revenue to the Government and the military aristocracy. This military aristocracy was composed of Afghán *Jágírdárs*, who held their lands or *Jágírs* on the system explained at page 43; and who maintained a considerable number of rapacious and often lawless followers who disdained all kind of labour except that of a soldier. The harshness with which the Afghán authorities used to collect the revenue is shown by all the historians of the Afgháns; one of the best of whom, the author of the *Tárikh-i-Firúz-Sháhí*, says:—" When the collector of the Díwán asks them (the Hindús) to pay the tax, they should pay it with all humility and submission. And if the collector wishes to spit into their mouths, they should open their mouths without the slightest fear of contamination so that the collector may do so. In this state, with their mouths open, they should stand before the collector. The object of such humiliations and spitting into their mouths is to prove the obedience of infidel subjects under protection.*
In time of war the Afghán armies occupied the country much as if it were the land of an open enemy; and as, after the death of Isá [see § 4] they plundered the lands of the temple of Jagannáth in Púrí, so at all times no considerations of religion ever interfered with their plundering propensities.

The condition of the Hindús of Bengal vastly improved under the Mughuls during these early times, mainly owing to the impartial and tolerant policy of Akbar; who (as we have seen in the cases of the Rájás Todar Mall and Mán Singh) chose his advisers and generals only because of their qualifications, and with no regard to their religion or their race. On the whole,

---

* This passage is quoted from the *Tarikh-i-Firúz Sháhí*, p. 290.

the suppression of the Afghán power by the Mughuls may be considered to have been a blessing to the greater portion of the inhabitants of Bengal. At a later period of the history, however, we shall see that some of the Mughul Nawábs rivalled the earlier Afgháns in their profligacy and their oppressions; so that the establishment of the British rule, always kind and equitable, though firm and vigorous, was really the greatest blessing that has ever happened to this country.

§ 9. *The Portuguese Wars in Bengal.*—It was during the reign of Islám Khán, the conqueror of the Afgháns, that the Portuguese first began to attract notice in Bengal. The first act of Islám Khán's authority was to transfer the capital of the province from Rájmahall in the north, to Dacca in the south-east; and the reason assigned for this transfer was the Súbahdár's desire to be near the scene of the inroads of the Portuguese and Mughs or Arakanese.

The Portuguese had established themselves on the west coast of India during the first years of the 16th century. As early as 1537-38 their vessels had visited the Ganges; and at the time of which we are speaking, large numbers of them had settled on the coasts of Arakán and Chittagong, subsisting for the most part on the plunder of the neighbouring coast of Bengal. The most important body of these Portuguese pirates, for they were really no better than pirates, had seized and fortified the islands of Sondíp and Dakhin Shahbázpur at the mouth of the Megna (the river formed by the junction of the Brahmaputra and the Ganges) under the leadership of one *Sebastian Gonzales*, who had formerly been only a common sailor, but who was elected chief of these freebooters. Gonzales now, allied with the Rájá of Arakán and his subjects the Maghs, invaded Bengal in 1610, under the agreement that all conquests should be equally divided between the Maghs and the Portuguese. The allies however were defeated by the vigour of Islám Khán, who pursued them nearly as far as Chittagong; and this fortunate victory gave the Mughul Subáhdár sufficient strength to complete the conquest of the Afgháns, as described in the last section.

On the death of Islám Khán in 1613, he was succeeded by his

brother Kásim Khán. During his reign the Portuguese pirates, through the treachery of Gonzales, quarreled with the Rájá of Arakán, seized his fleet, and plundered the coasts of Arakán; and even invited their countryman, the viceroy of the Portuguese possessions in India, who lived at Goa, to aid them in conquering the whole country of Arakán. The Rájá, however, got assistance from some Dutch ships, and succeeded in beating off the Portuguese; and ultimately invaded Sondíp, utterly defeated Gonzales and drove him away. The Maghs now began to plunder Bengal; at which the emperor Jáhangír was so angry that he dismissed the Súbahdár Kásim Khán, and appointed in his place Ibráhím Khán, the brother of the empress Nur Jahán, A.D. 1618.

To conclude the history of the Portuguese in Bengal, we shall here omit the reigns of the next five Súbahdárs, returning to them in the next section; and we now pass on to *Kásim Khán Juwainí* (not related to the Kásim Khán of whom we have just been speaking) who was appointed Governor of Bengal by Sháh Jahán in 1628, immediately after the accession of the latter to the throne of Dehli. Of late years the Portuguese had largely extended their power in Bengal, possessing two strong settlements, one at Hugli, the other at Chittagong. Sháh Jahán, whilst prince, had governed Bengal [*see* next section] and had been very angry at the practices of the Portuguese, who were in the habit of forcing the natives to become Christians; so he ordered Kásim to destroy their settlement utterly. In February 1632, Kásim sent a strong army against Hugli under his son Ináyatullah. The Portuguese defended themselves with valour, and slew numbers of the besiegers; and for several months they held out. At last the Mughuls succeeded in laying dry the ditch in front of the church, dug a mine under it and blew it up; and the town and fort were taken, on September 10, 1632. More than four thousand prisoners were captured; and the Portuguese never again recovered their power in Bengal. Hugli was made a royal port by the Mughuls, and rapidly became a great and prosperous city; attracting all the trade of Sátganw, which declined from this time.

§ 10. *Ibráhím Khán and the Rebellion of Sháh Jahán.*—We

CHAP. VI.] THE MUHAMMADAN RULE IN BENGAL. 53

must now return to the history of the five Súbahdárs whose reigns intervened between those of the first Kásim Khán and Kásim Khán Juwainí.

Ibráhím Khán Fath-jang was the fourth son of Ghiyás Beg, and younger brother of the empress Núr Jahán. As his family were all powerful at the Court of Agra, he ruled Bengal in great power and prosperity. Agriculture and commerce were encouraged; and as the empress had entirely changed the fashion of ladies' dresses, and caused them to wear all manner of dresses of delicate and expensive texture, the manufactures of Bengal were carried to a high state of perfection—for the fine muslin cloths manufactured at Dacca (of which many yards could be drawn through a small ring), and the silks of Máldah, supplied clothes for all the courtiers of Agra.

A further impetus was given to the commerce of Bengal by the arrival of the first English merchants, who temporarily established a factory at Patná in 1620 [see § 12].

Now that the attacks of the Afgháns, of the Portuguese, and the Maghs, had all been successfully repelled, there appeared a reasonable hope that Bengal might long enjoy this unwonted peace and prosperity. But the rebellion of the Prince Sháh Jahán against his father, the Emperor Jahángír, soon again filled the country with bloodshed and rapine. Sháh Jahán had attained a very high reputation by his successful wars in the Dakhin; till at length, in the year 1631, finding that the succession to the Empire was likely to be given to his elder brother, he determined to use the Mughul army of the Dakhin to rebel against his father and enforce his own succession. Being defeated in the Dakhin, he formed the bold resolution of invading Bengal, so as to possess himself of the great wealth and resources of that country, wherewith to carry on the rebellion. He marched through Talingánah to Orissa, of which he obtained quiet possession; and refreshed his troops by a rest at Katak. He then advanced into Bengal, and took Bardwán by storm; and demanded aid from the Portuguese Governor, which however was refused [see last section]. The prince then marched to attack the Súbahdár Ibráhím Khán; who had fortified the pass of Teliágarhí [see Chap. I., § 3], and seized all the boats on the Ganges so as to prevent Sháh Jahán from crossing the Ganges to avoid Teliágarhí. Ibráhím posted himself with part of his army on the banks of the Ganges opposite to Teliágarhí, where he believed himself safe from the attack of Sháh Jahán; but the latter, having obtained boats from some zamíndárs of Bhágalpur, crossed the river and fell on Ibráhím's army with great fury. When Ibráhím saw that the battle was going against him, he exclaimed, " my life is of no value, I will devote it to the service of His Majesty the Emperor, and either conquer or die!" So saying, he rushed into the thickest of the fight, and fell covered with wounds. The fort at Teliágarhí was captured by the Prince's officers on the same day; and Sháh Jahán was now master of Bengal. He employed the two years, during which he remained in possession of the province, in collecting as much treasure and as many men and elephants as possible, to carry on the war against his father; and he also succeeded in seizing the impregnable fortress of Rahtás, in which he placed his family. He was however defeated at length by the Emperor's forces on the banks of the Tons; and finally, being reduced to great distress, had to throw himself on the mercy of his father. Jahángír forgave him; but he had to give up all the places in his possession; and Mahábat Khán (the General who had defeated him) was appointed to succeed him as Governor of Bengal—Khánah-zád Khán, the son of Mahábat, being deputy and ruling for his father.

The short reigns (1624—1628) of the three Governors who came after Sháh Jahán—Khánahzad Khán, Mukarram Khán, and Fidáí Khán—were not marked by any events of importance; and the history of the reign of Kásim Khán Juwainí, 1628—1632, has been given in § 9.

§ 11. *Islám Khán Mashhadí.*—Kásim Khán Juwainí was succeeded by Azím Khán in 1632; but as it was found that he did not possess sufficient ability or courage to defend his province from the Maghs and Assamese who frequently made incursions, he was superseded in 1637 by *Islám Khán Mashhadí.*

In the following year, 1638, the Magh Governor of Chittagong, named Mukat Rái, came and offered to hold the territory of

CHAP. VI.] THE MUHAMMADAN RULE IN BENGAL. 55

Chittagong as a vassal of the Mughul Emperor instead of the Rájá of Arakán. Islám Khán accepted his offer; and changed the name of the town to Islámábad—by which name it is still known to Muhammadans. Chittagong however was not finally attached to the Mughul Empire until twenty-eight years later. In the same year the Assamese invaded Bengal with a large army; they plundered all the towns on the banks of the Megná, and had nearly reached Dacca, when they were met and defeated by the Súbahdár. Islám Khán in revenge entered Assam, and took many forts; he also overran part of Koch Bihár; but had to retire at the approach of the rainy season. Soon afterwards he was recalled to Agra, to become Vazír of the Mughul Empire. His conquests were completed by Mír Júmlah, many years afterwards.

§ 12. *The First Settlement of the English in Bengal.*—Sultán Shujá, the second son of the Emperor Sháh Jahán, was appointed to succeed Islám Khán as Súbahdár of Bengal; and immediately transferred the capital of Bengal from Dacca to Rájmahall once more. During his long reign of twenty-two years, the English obtained a firm footing as traders in Bengal; but we must go back a little to trace their earliest history here.

In the year 1600 the great English Queen, Elizabeth, granted permission to some of her subjects to form a Company for the purpose of trading to India and the East. This Company was afterwards the famous EAST INDIA COMPANY; which ruled a great part of India until 1858, when Her Gracious Majesty the present Queen of England, Victoria, took the government into her own hands. The East India Company at first traded chiefly with the west coast of India, especially at the port of Súrat, and with the islands of the Eastern Archipelago. But as early as 1611, some of the Company's vessels visited the coasts of Bengal, at a port called Piplí, near Balasor.

[NOTE.—Piplí or Sháhbandar is now no longer on the sea-coast, but on the Súbanrekhá; this is owing to the fact that much land has been formed between it and the sea.]

It has already been mentioned [§ 10] that during the time of Ibráhím Khán, about 1620, the English for a short time set up a factory at Patna. This only lasted about a year; but in 1634, during the brief reign of Azím Khán, the Company obtained a *Farmán*, or imperial edict, from the Emperor Sháh Jahán, allowing them to erect a permanent factory in Piplí.

Whilst the Sultán Shujá was Súbahdár of Bengal (1638—1661) a fortunate accident enabled the English Company largely to extend their trading operations throughout India, and especially in Bengal. It happened that one of the daughters of the Emperor Sháh Jahán was dreadfully burnt one day, by her clothes catching fire; an express was sent to the English factory at Súrat for an English Surgeon; and Mr. Boughton quickly proceeded to the imperial camp, and soon cured the young Princess. The Emperor offered Mr. Boughton any reward he liked to name; and the latter requested and obtained permission for his countrymen to carry on trade in Bengal free of all duties or taxes, A.D. 1636. Mr. Boughton then went to Prince Shujá with this order, and was favourably received by him, and allowed to extend the trade of the English factory at Piplí. Shortly afterwards it happened that one of the ladies of Sultán Shujá's háram was taken ill; Mr. Boughton was summoned to attend her, and was as fortunate as before in effecting a cure, A.D. 1639. From this time, the favour shown to the English by the Sultán was unbounded; they were allowed to erect factories at Huglí and Balasor, and to export and import goods free of duty—especially to export large quantities of saltpetre, which at that time was an article of great value.

§ 13. *Condition of the people under Sultán Shujá.*—Sultán Shujá governed Bengal for about twenty-two years, with the exception of two years during which he was sent as Governor to Kábul. During the first eighteen years of this period, from 1639 to 1657, the province enjoyed profound peace; and consequently attained to a pitch of prosperity unknown since the first Muhammadan conquest. The people were secured from foreign invasion by the fact that their Governor was the son of the mighty Mughul Emperor; and they were protected from domestic oppression by his impartial administration of justice, whilst the country flourished both in commerce and in agriculture under the encouragement which he wisely gave to industry. The frontiers of Bengal had of late been considerably extended; and Shujá, shortly before 1658, drew up a new rent-roll, showing a total revenue of more than one crore and thirty-one lakhs of rupees. Thus the revenue had increased since the time of Akbar [see § 2] by more than twenty-four lakhs.

§ 14. *Shujá's attempt on the Empire.*—But the contest for the empire of Hindústán, which occurred as soon as the great Sháh Jahán became dangerously ill, produced just the same effects on Bengal as those which we have described when Sháh Jahán himself aspired to the empire during the life of his father Jahángír [see § 10].

In 1657 the illness of the Emperor Sháh Jahán became known to his younger sons; although the eldest, Prince Dárá, endeavoured to conceal it. Shujá immediately prepared to march against Dárá, to secure the throne for himself; but was met near Banáras by Prince Sulaimán, the son of Dárá (1658), and being taken by surprise in the midst of some negociations, was compelled to fly with the loss of all his baggage, treasures, and elephants, and to take refuge in the fortress of Munger.

Meanwhile the two other sons of Sháh Jahán, Aurangzeb and Murád, had joined their forces; and had secured the assistance of Mír Júmlah, the greatest of the Mughul generals. Sulaimán was recalled by his father Prince Dárá to aid him against these new enemies. A great battle was fought near Agra, in which Dárá was defeated; and the subsequent treachery of Aurangzeb against Murád gave the former full possession of the Imperial throne.

Shujá thought it prudent at first to conciliate Aurangzeb; but at length marched on Allahábád to claim the empire. Near this place another great battle was fought with the imperial forces under Aurangzeb and Mír Júmlah; and here, as in the battle of Banáras, Shujá allowed himself to be surprised, and suffered a total defeat, A.D. 1659. He was pursued by Mír Júmlah and Prince Muhammad, son of Aurangzeb, to Rájmahall, whence he was compelled to fly to Tándah; and the rains setting in, he remained at Tándah, whilst Mír Júmlah occupied Rájmahall for several months.

During this interval a remarkable and interesting event happened, which at one time seemed likely to retrieve Shujá's fortunes. The young son of Aurangzeb, Prince Muhammad, who was now associated with Mír Júmlah as commander of the imperial army, had been betrothed to a beautiful daughter of the Sultán Shujá before the outbreak of the war between Shujá and Aurangzeb. The betrothal had been almost forgotten during the progress of the war; and even if remembered, it was regarded as having been broken off by the quarrel between the parents of the lovers. But whilst Shujá was now shut up in Tándah, the young Princess, his daughter, wrote a pathetic letter with her own hand to her former lover. The Prince was a young man of a generous disposition, and was touched with pity at the misery of the beautiful damsel whom he had formerly promised to make his wife. He determined to desert his father's cause and take up that of his uncle Shujá; and he endeavoured to induce the army also to desert Aurangzeb. He accordingly joined Shujá at Tándah, and his nuptials were celebrated with great pomp and rejoicings; but Mír Júmlah not only prevented the army from following the example of Prince Muhammad, but also prepared immediately to attack Shujá and his new son-in-law. A decisive battle was fought outside the walls of Tándah; and Shujá and Muhammad, utterly routed, were compelled to fly to Dacca. Subsequently (A.D. 1660) an artifice of Aurangzeb, who wrote a friendly letter to Muhammad so that it might be intercepted, caused Shujá to suspect his son-in-law of treachery, and to dismiss him; and the unhappy young Prince, falling into the hands of his ruthless father, was condemned to pine away many years of his life in the great prison-fortress of Gwáliár. Shujá ultimately was driven into Arakán, where he was shamefully ill-treated by the Rájá, who demanded his daughter in marriage; and at length was taken prisoner and drowned, A. D. 1661. His wife and two of his daughters committed suicide; the third daughter was forcibly married to the Rájá. No prince was ever more beloved than the unfortunate Shujá; but he had neither the energy nor the ability to contend with such an enemy as Aurangzeb.

§ 15. *Mír Júmlah.*—The great General Mír Júmlah, having

CHAP. VI.] THE MUHAMMADAN RULE IN BENGAL. 59

been appointed Governor of Bengal by Aurangzeb for the purpose of extinguishing the hopes of Shujá, made Dacca his capital; and for nearly thirteen years he governed the province with vigour and success. He determined to punish the Assamese for their frequent invasions of Bengal; and assembled a large army for that purpose in 1661. He first overran Koch Bihár, and seized its capital, which he called Alamgírnagar in honour of his imperial master (Alamgír is another name of Aurangzeb). In the following year, 1662, he marched up the banks of the Brahmaputra, and finally captured Ghargáon, which was then the capital.

[NOTE.—The site of Ghargáon is now occupied by a place called Nazirah near Síbságar, one of the chief civil stations of Assam.]

From Ghargáon he wrote to the Emperor Aurangzeb that he had conquered the road to China, and that he intended in the following year to invade that vast and almost unknown country. During the year however numerous disasters from floods and pestilence overtook the Mughul army; and Mír Júmlah at last thought it prudent to retreat. By the time he reached Gauháti on the march back, most of his soldiers were incapacitated by disease or fatigue; nevertheless he sent off from that place a strong detachment to reconquer Koch Bihár, which had revolted on hearing of the sufferings of the Mughul army. Shortly after his return to Dacca, Mír Júmlah died, overcome by the anxieties of the expedition and by the bad effects of the climate of Assam, A.D. 1664. It was generally believed that the Emperor Aurangzeb was glad to hear of his death, as he was jealous of his power and reputation.

§ 16. *Sháistah Khán.* — The Emperor appointed Sháistah Khán to be the next Governor of Bengal, who was the nephew of the Empress Núr Jahán, son of Asaf Jáh, and therefore brother of the Empress Mumtáz Mahall. With the exception of the short interval between 1676 and 1679, when Fidái Khán and the Sultán Muhammad Azím (third son of Aurangzeb) were successively governors, he ruled Bengal from 1664 to 1689. During his reign the Dutch, French, and Danes established important factories in Bengal—the Dutch at Chinsurah, the French at Chandernagar, and the Danes at Serampur. The chief English factory in Bengal was unfortunately placed in the midst of the great native city of Huglí; and this was the cause of numerous disturbances during the time of Sháistah Khán, and at last resulted in the temporary abandonment of the country by the English.

The Rájá of Arakán, emboldened by the impunity with which he had ill-treated the unfortunate Shujá, and hearing of the misfortunes of Mír Júmlah in Assam, began to plunder the Bengal territories about the mouths of the Megna and the Ganges. He also encouraged the Portuguese vagabonds,* who were very numerous in his dominions, to commit the greatest atrocities on the unoffending inhabitants of the Bengal coasts and river-banks. Sháistah Khán accordingly determined to invade Arakán; and first of all, he induced the Portuguese, partly by threats and partly by promises, to desert the Rájá. From these he selected the most suitable for his army; and the rest he settled at a place, since called Firingí Bázár, near Dacca. He then marched against Arakán, and completely subdued the territory of Chittagong, which he finally annexed to Bengal, A.D. 1666.

§ 17. *Sháistah Khán's quarrel with the English Merchants.*— During the three years that Sháistah Khán was absent from Bengal, Fidái Khán and the Sultán Muhammad Azím were successively governors of Bengal, from 1676 to 1679; and in 1677 the English merchants had obtained a perpetual *Farmán* from the Emperor Aurangzeb, giving them great privileges of trade in Bengal with only the small annual payment of 3,000 rupees. In consequence of this, the East India Company determined to make their settlements in Bengal independent (they had formerly been subordinate to the Government of Madras): and they sent out Mr. Hedges in 1681 as the first Governor of the Bengal factories. They then possessed extensive factories or trading-houses at Huglí, Patna, Dacca, and Kásimbazár near Murshidábád. The Governor or chief agent resided at Huglí; and though

---

* These were for the most part escaped criminals, murderers and the like, who had run away from Goa and the other Portuguese possessions in India, and taken refuge in Arakán.

CHAP. VI.] THE MUHAMMADAN RULE IN BENGAL. 61

he had no fortress, yet he was allowed a small guard of English soldiers to give dignity to his office.

The quarrel between Sháistah Khán and the English merchants sprang originally from insignificant causes. In the year 1682, a rebellion occurred in Bihár, which was soon suppressed; but for a short time the rebels had been sufficiently strong to besiege the city of Patna—and during this siege, the English factory near Patna had been uninjured by the rebels. On this account the Súbahdár suspected the English of having been implicated in the rebellion; and consequently put a stop to their trade for that year, notwithstanding the Emperor's *Farmán*. Again in 1685, the English requested permission to erect a small fort near the mouth of the Ganges, to prevent other English ships, not connected with the East India Company, from sailing up the river. The Súbahdár not only refused to grant this request, but, to punish the merchants for making it, he ordered that they should in future pay a heavy duty on their trade, instead of the 3,000 rupees ordered by the Emperor. He also wrote to the Emperor Aurangzeb to influence him against the English ; and at length the Company were so exasperated that they obtained permission from King James II. of England to make war against Sháistah Khán, and if necessary against the Emperor Aurangzeb himself. This war, which was foolishly determined on by the Company, was never carried on with spirit; for those merchants who were resident in the country were generally anxious to live on terms of peace with the natives, by which means alone they saw that they could carry on trade to advantage.

A fleet of ships was sent out in 1686 by the East India Company, with orders to conquer Chittagong and erect a strong fortress there, and afterwards to attack the Nawáb at Dacca and force him to make restitution to the English merchants. Admiral Nicholson was in command of this fleet; but his ships were dispersed by tempests, and part of them by mistake entered the western arm of the Ganges and proceeded to Huglí. About this time a street-quarrel in the town of Huglí between some English soldiers and the Nawáb's troops ended in the *Bombardment of Huglí* by the English ships (1686). In this bombardment a large quantity of property, including the factory belonging to the English merchants, was destroyed; and to revenge this outrage, the Nawáb immediately seized all the other English factories at Patna, Máldah, Dacca, and Kásimbazár, and ordered a powerful army to march against Huglí. Mr. *Charnock*, famous to this day as the founder of Calcutta, was at this time Governor of the English settlements in Bengal; and he, thinking that Huglí was an insecure position, ordered all the English to remove to a village called "Chuttanutty," part of the present site of Calcutta, because that place could be protected by the English ships in the river. This was in 1686; which therefore may be considered the date of the founding of Calcutta. Early in the next year, however, Mr. Charnock determined to retreat to a position lower down the river; so the English took up their position at *Hijlí*, a very unhealthy position at the mouth of the Huglí river. A short peace with the Nawáb followed, during which Mr. Charnock and his followers returned to Calcutta; but new quarrels soon arose, and the affairs of the English in Bengal were well-nigh ruined by the rashness and violent temper of *Captain Heath*, who arrived from England in 1688. This officer, not considering the ill-effects that must result from such violence, in estranging the minds of the natives from the English merchants, first ordered all the English to embark on board his ships, and then proceed to attack the rich town of Balasor: where he captured a battery of thirty guns, and sacked the city. After this he made an abortive attempt on Chittagong; and then, without waiting for the Nawáb's answer to some proposals he had made for peace, he sailed away to Madras with all the English merchants on board his ships. Thus Bengal was entirely abandoned for a time by the English, A.D. 1689.

It was about this time that the Nawáb Sháistah Khán resigned the government of Bengal. His conduct to Europeans appears to have been sometimes harsh; but it must be admitted that he received many provocations from them, and that the behaviour of the European traders in the country was very often arrogant and insulting. The memory of Sháistah Khán has always been held in respect by his own countrymen. It is related of him that,

CHAP. VI.] THE MUHAMMADAN RULE IN BENGAL. 63

when rice was so cheap as to be sold at the rate of eight *mans*, (320 *seers*) for the rupee, he ordered the gate of Dacca through which he passed on his departure to be closed and built up, and never to be opened by any of his successors until rice again became so cheap [*see* § 26].

§ 18. *The Nawáb Ibráhím Khán; the rebellion of Sobhá Singh, and the fortification of Calcutta by the English.*—Sháistah Khán was succeeded in the government of Bengal by the Nawáb Ibráhím Khán, who was appointed by Aurangzeb in 1689. He was a man of no military talents; but he loved to encourage agriculture and commerce, and he was consequently very glad to receive, in the following year, 1690, an order from the Emperor Aurangzeb, authorising him to invite the English merchants to return from Madras to Bengal. The English ships of war had been capturing many ships belonging to the Mughuls on the various coasts of India, and had also prevented the Muhammadan pilgrims from going in ships from India to Mecca; so that Aurangzeb was very anxious to become friendly with the English again. Mr. Charnock at first refused to return to Bengal, unless very large concessions were made to the English; but at length he and all the merchants and officers of the settlement came back in 1690; and the next year (1691) they received a *Hasbulhuqam*, or imperial order, from Aurangzeb, authorising the English to carry on trade in Bengal free of all customs or duties, except the payment of a *peshkash* of 3,000 rupees yearly. Twice during the next four years the trade of Calcutta was threatened with serious interruption: the first time was in 1692, when the Sultán of Turkey in Europe requested the Emperor Aurangzeb to prevent Europeans from exporting saltpetre,* on the ground that they used it in making gunpowder wherewith to fight against the Muhammadan subjects of the Sultán of the Turks; the second time was in 1695, when Captain Kyd, a famous English pirate,† captured a number of Mughul ships, including two pilgrim-vessels

---

* Saltpetre was at this time one of the principal exports from Bengal.

† Captain Kyd captured the ships and plundered the property of his own countrymen quite as readily as those of other nations.

going from India to Arabia. On each of these occasions, the Emperor Aurangzeb was very angry with the English, and ordered their trade to be stopped; but the favour of the Nawáb Ibráhím Khán enabled them to carry it on.

The English merchants in Bengal, however, had long observed that the merchants of Bombay and Madras were able to carry on their trade in security even when the Emperor was angry with them, because Bombay was a fortified island, and Madras possessed a strong fortress; so they were very anxious to build a fortress at Calcutta. Neither the Emperor, nor the Nawáb, was willing to allow them to do this; but at last a fortunate combination of circumstances enabled them to erect "Fort William" in 1696-1697. It happened in the following way. In the year 1696 a Hindú zamíndár of the Bardwán district, named *Sobhá Singh*, had some grievance against the Rájá of Bardwán who was called Rájá Krishna Rám; so he got together some troops, and being joined by a number of discontented Afgháns under Rahím Khán, he raised a serious insurrection. He reached Bardwán, killed the Rájá, and overran all the surrounding country; and at length besieged and took Huglí, driving out the Faujdár* of Huglí, who ran away to get assistance from the Nawáb.

As soon as the rebellion became serious, the English at Calcutta (and also the Dutch at Chinsurah and the French at Chandernagar) asked the Nawáb that they might be allowed, as friends of the Government and enemies of the rebels, to fortify their factories. The Nawáb told them to "defend themselves;" so with great alacrity they proceeded to build the long-wished-for fortress; and as King William the Third was then King of England, they called it "Fort William."

Hugli was soon retaken by the troops of the Nawáb, by the aid of the Dutch of Chinsurah; and Sobhá Singh returned to Bardwán, whilst his followers proceeded to overrun Nadiyá and Murshidábád under Rahím Khán. The end of Sobhá Singh was

---

* The *Faujdár* under the Muhammadan Governments in India was the head of the police and the chief military officer of a district.

tragical, and is a well-known story. At the time of his sacking Bardwán and killing the Rájá, he had captured the Rájá's daughter, a young damsel famous alike for her beauty and her virtue; and the vile wretch had kept her in close confinement ever since. On his return to Bardwán, he attempted to offer her violence; but the heroic girl drew a long sharp knife which she had kept secreted under her dress, and first stabbed the villain to the heart, and then plunged the dagger into her own bosom.

After the death of Sobhá Singh, the rebels elected Rahím Khán as their Chief; and, owing to the extraordinary apathy of the Nawáb Ibráhím Khán, managed to make themselves masters of all Western Bengal, from Rájmahall to Midnapur. At length the Emperor Aurangzeb superseded Ibráhím in 1696, and appointed his own grandson Prince Azim-us-Shán (son of the Sultán Muazzam, afterwards Bahádúr Sháh or Sháh Alam I.) to be Governor of Bengal. Before the arrival of the Prince Azim, a brave and active son of Ibráhím, named Zabardast Khán, had done something to atone for his father's feebleness, by defeating the rebels in a decisive battle near Rájmahall, A.D. 1697; but the insurrection was not entirely suppressed until 1698, when Rahím Khán, after treacherously assassinating the envoy of Prince Azim, was defeated and slain in a battle near Bardwán, and of his followers some were killed and others entered the service of the prince.

§ 19. *Sultán Azim-us-Shán; the English allowed to purchase the Zamíndári of Calcutta.*—The Prince Azím-us-Shán, grandson of the Emperor Aurangzeb and son of the Emperor Bahádúr Sháh, governed Bengal nominally from his appointment in 1696 till his death in 1712; but his reign virtually ended in 1706, when he left the province in order to assist his father Bahádúr Sháh in securing the throne of Dehli. The most important event of his reign was the grant of largely increased privileges to the English merchants of Calcutta, in the year 1698. By the payment of a large sum of money to the Prince, they obtained permission to purchase " the villages of Chuttanutty, Goviudpur, and Calcutta " from the zamíndár who formerly held them; and from this time the East India Company were the possessors of territory in Bengal—though of course as yet in strict subjection to the Nawáb.

§ 20. *The union of the Old and New East India Companies.*—In the same year that the Old East India Company acquired the zamíndárí of Calcutta, a new Company was started in England with the favour of the King of England; and this was the cause of much quarrelling amongst the English merchants, and also of the failure of an embassy that was sent under Sir William Norris by the King of England to the Emperor Aurangzeb in 1701-2. Whilst the ambassador Sir William Norris was with the Emperor Aurangzeb in his camp in the Dakhin, news arrived that some Mughul ships had been captured by English pirates; the ambassador was required to give a guarantee that this should not happen again; but refusing to do so, he left the country in disgust. Aurangzeb, in anger at this, ordered all Europeans in his dominions to be seized and put into prison; but Mr. Beard, the President of the English Factory at Calcutta, prepared to defend his fort—and shortly afterwards the Emperor consented to allow the English trade to go on as before. In 1706—1708 the two English Companies were united under the title of *the United Company of Merchants trading to the East Indies;* and the whole of the property of both Companies being brought into Fort William, its garrison was augmented to the number of 130 European soldiers, and a number of cannons were mounted on the ramparts. This gave great confidence to the native merchants, who now resorted to Calcutta in vast numbers; so that the town soon became one of the richest and most populous in Bengal.

§ 21. *The Rise of Murshid Kulí Khán.*—Murshid Kulí Khán, who is sometimes also called Jafar Khán, is said to have been originally the son of a poor Bráhman, sold in infancy to a Persian merchant, who brought him up as a Muhammadan. By his energy in business affairs, he had risen to be Díwán of Haidarábád under the Emperor Aurangzeb; and in 1701 he was appointed by the Emperor to be Díwán of Bengal, Prince Azim-us-Shán being still Názim.

CHAP. VI.] THE MUHAMMADAN RULE IN BENGAL. 67

[NOTE.—The two offices of *Názim* and *Díwán* of the various great provinces of the Empire were carefully kept distinct by Aurangzeb, so that no officer should become too powerful. The *Názim* was the Military Governor; his business was to defend the country both from external invasion and from internal insurrections, to act as head of the police, and enforce obedience to the laws: and under him were the Faujdárs of districts [*see* page 64]. The duty of the Díwán was to collect the revenue, and to superintend all expenditure. He was in a certain degree subject to the orders of the Názim, being obliged to supply the Názim with money for the service of Government, if the latter forwarded a written demand for it; but the Názim was responsible for making a proper use of the money thus supplied him by the Díwán; and the two great officers were ordered by the Mughul Emperors to consult together and act in harmony on all important occasions.]

Murshid Kulí Khán, as soon as he was appointed Díwán, induced the Emperor to annul all grants of Military *Jágírs* [*see* page 43] in Bengal, the jágídárs being compensated by having new jágírs assigned to them in Orissa and other districts not so fully settled and quiet as Bengal. In this and other ways he largely increased the revenues of the province, and grew more and more in the favour of the Emperor; but he greatly offended the Názim, Prince Azim-us-Shán. The latter tried, without success, to get him assassinated; at last the jealousy grew to an open quarrel, when the Emperor took the side of Murshid Kulí Khán and severely reprimanded the Prince. After this, Murshid resolved no longer to live in the same capital with Azim; so he left Dacca, and took up his abode at Makhsúsábád, the name of which city he altered some years afterwards to Murshídábád. At the same time the Prince was ordered by Aurangzeb to leave Bengal and go to Bíhár. In the following year, the Díwán visited the Emperor's camp in the Dakhin, and presented the accounts of the province in person, together with an immense present; he was consequently reappointed Díwán of Bengal, Bihár, and Orissa, and at the same time made Deputy Názim under Prince Azim in Bengal and Orissa.

§ 22. *Murshid Kulí Khán as Governor of Bengal.*—Prince Azim-us-Shán, after leaving Bengal in 1706, was mainly instrumental in placing his father Bahádúr Sháh on the throne of Hindústán. This he was able to effect partly by the troops that he brought with him from Bengal; but chiefly by the immense treasures that he carried away with him, with which he was able to employ other troops.

[NOTE.—It must be remembered that there were, at the time of which we are speaking, large numbers of troops scattered about in various parts of Northern India, ready to serve any one who had money to pay them. These soldiers provided their own horses and arms; and in addition to the pay which they got from their employers, they expected to be allowed to plunder the country of the enemy. The suppression of these mercenary bands of soldiers by the English rule was a great blessing to India.]

From the time when Prince Azim-us-Shán left Bengal in 1706, the Nawáb Murshid Kulí Khán was really Governor of Bengal. The Prince continued to be nominally the Názim, during the reign (five years) of his father Bahádúr Sháh at Dehli; and he even appointed his son Farrukh Siyar to be his Deputy during that period; but Farrukh Siyar, though he lived in the palace at Murshidábád, in no way meddled with the affairs of government, leaving all to the Díwán Murshid.

[NOTE.—After the death of Bahádúr Sháh in 1712, Prince Azim-us-Shán was slain in the contest for the Empire; and his elder brother became Emperor under the title of Jahándár Sháh, having slain all his relations, except Farrukh Siyar, who was safe in Bengal. Farrukh Siyar asked Murshid Kulí Khán to assist him in killing Jahándár; but the Díwán refused, and Farrukh Siyar left Bengal. Ultimately, however, he obtained the assistance of the two famous Sayyids, Husain Alí, Governor of Bihár, and his brother Abdullah, Governor of Allahábád; and in the battle of Agra, defeated and slew Jahándár, and succeeded to the throne of Dehli as the Emperor Farrukh Siyar.]

During all these contests for the Empire of Hindústán, Murshid Kulí Khán remained quiet and strengthened his government in Bengal; regularly sending a large revenue to the reigning Emperor of Dehli, whoever he might be, and in this way retaining the favour of all the successive Emperors. In the course of less than sixteen years, he is said to have sent no less than 16½ crores of rupees to Dehli.

We have stated [§ 21] that Murshid, shortly after his appointment as Díwán, induced the Emperor to annul most of the grants of Jágírs in Bengal, thus taking the collection of the revenue more directly into the hands of the Government. Gradually he drew up a new rent-roll, which was the third that had been drawn up since the Mughul conquest—the first [see § 2] having been completed by Rájá Todar Mall in 1582; and the second by Sultán Shujá in 1658. Murshid's rent-roll was completed in 1722, and was called the *Kámil Jama Túmárí* or "Perfect Rent-roll;" in which Bengal was divided into 34 Sirkárs, forming 13 *Chaklahs*, and subdivided into 1660 *Parganahs*, with a total revenue of Rupees 14,288,186—or more than one crore and forty-two lakhs, showing a further increase on Shujá's revenue of more than eleven lakhs.

This enormous revenue was collected by the Díwán and his subordinate officers in the díwání department,* directly from the great zamíndárs, who in their turn collected it from the ryots; but before he made over the collection of the revenue to the zamíndárs, he caused all the lands to be remeasured, and a large quantity of waste lands to be brought under cultivation by ryots who held these lands directly from the Government. Murshid Kulí Khán, who was generally very just and impartial in his government, was however very rigorous and even extortionate in the collection of the revenue; and he allowed such frightful oppression of his Hindú subjects by the subordinate *díwání* officers, that his name is detested by the Hindús to the present day. Notwithstanding this, he preferred to employ Hindús in the subordinate posts of the *díwání* department, because they were more docile than Muhammadans, and more skilled in keeping accounts.

Many stories are told to illustrate the severity of Murshid Kulí Khán in revenue matters, especially to his Hindú subjects. One of the principal agents of his oppression was the Násir Ahmad, to whom he used to deliver up any zamíndárs who were in arrears, to be tormented by every species of cruelty; such as hanging them up by the feet; the bastinado;† setting them in

* That is, the department that collected and administered the revenue.
† The Bastinado consisted in beating, with bamboos, the soles of the feet or the stomachs of the unfortunate prisoners.

the sun in summer time; stripping them naked and sprinkling them with cold water in winter. But the most disgusting cruelty was that of Sayyid Rezá Khán, who had married the granddaughter of the Nawáb, and who was made Deputy-Díwán of Bengal. He ordered a tank to be dug, and filled with ordure and everything filthy that could be thought of; and if the zamíndárs were still unwilling or unable to pay their arrears of revenue after having suffered all the other punishments, they were stripped naked and dragged repeatedly through this filthy pond by a rope tied under their arms. This tank he ironically named *Baikúnt* or *Paradise*.

On the accession of Farrukh Siyar to the throne of Dehli in 1713, Murshid Kulí Khán was appointed both Názim and Díwán—thus uniting the two offices which had been separated since the time of Akbar. He was very strict in his religious observances; and devoted two days in the week to the administration of justice, personally sitting in the Court; and so rigorously impartial was he in his decisions, that on one occasion he sentenced his own son to death. He maintained great state in his Court; no one was allowed to speak to another in his presence; and he even ordered that Hindú zamíndárs should not be allowed to ride in pálkís, but should be restricted to *dhúlís*. The Rájás of Tiparah, Koch Bihár, and Assam, though they still maintained an appearance of independence, were so much impressed by the power and abilities of the Nawáb, that they annually sent him valuable presents, and received in return *khilats*—thereby acknowledging his superiority.

§ 23. *Surgeon Hamilton, and the English Embassy to Dehli.*— The Nawáb greatly encouraged the foreign trade of Bengal, especially that which was in the hands of Mughul and Arab merchants. But he was extremely jealous of the political power which the English possessed owing to the possession of a strong fort at Calcutta, and to the *farmáns* they had obtained from the Emperors of Dehli. At last, in 1713, when he became both Názim and Díwán, he ordered that the English merchants should pay the usual duties on their merchandize. In consequence of this the East India Company sent an embassy to the Emperor Farrukh

Siyar. As the Nawáb was highly esteemed at Court on account of the regularity with which he transmitted the revenue, it is probable that no good would have resulted to the Company from this embassy, had it not been for a fortunate accident very similar to that one [*see* § 12] which had first obtained for them a footing in Bengal. Whilst the embassy was at Dehli, it happened that the Emperor's marriage with a beautiful Rájpút princess was delayed by his sickness; and in this difficulty, the services of Dr. Hamilton, the surgeon of the British Embassy, were asked for. The doctor quickly cured the emperor, and was told to name his own reward; and with rare disinterestedness, he (like Mr. Boughton long before) asked that the Emperor would grant the requests of the Embassy. These were, that the Company should be allowed to trade free of duty in Bengal; that they should have permission to purchase 38 villages in the neighbourhood of Calcutta; that the mint at Murshidábád should coin rupees for them on three days in the week: and that all persons indebted to the Company should be delivered up to them by the Nawáb's government. After many delays, the patent conceding these privileges was signed by Farrukh Siyar; and the embassy returned in triumph to Bengal. The Nawáb succeeded in preventing the Company from availing themselves of the Emperor's permission to purchase the 38 villages, by strictly charging the zamíndárs not to sell the land; but the other privileges were of immense value to the English merchants, and Calcutta grew in wealth and size more rapidly than ever.

§ 24. *Nawáb Shujá-ud-dín.*—The Nawáb Murshid Kulí Khán had in 1718 been made Governor of Bihár as well as of Bengal and Orissa; and when in 1719, Muhammad Sháh had succeeded to the throne of Dehli after the assassination of Farrukh Siyar and the deaths of his two successors, the new Emperor confirmed the Nawáb in all his appointments.

Shujá-ud-dín was an Afghán soldier of fortune who had married the only daughter of Murshid Kulí Khán. She had borne him a son to whom the title of Sarfaráz Khán had been given; and the old Nawáb had declared Sarfaráz Khán his heir. But Shujá managed, whilst acting as Deputy-Governor of Orissa under his father-in-law, secretly to get a patent from the Emperor Muhammad Sháh, declaring him Deputy-Governor; one of Muhammad's great courtiers being nominally Governor. On the death of Murshid Kulí Khán, Shujá succeeded him without any disturbance, and Sarfaráz Khán was pacified by being made Díwán of Bengal.

Shujá began his reign by an act which brought him much popularity amongst his Hindú subjects; for he set at liberty all those zamíndárs who had been imprisoned by the late Nawáb for arrears of revenue. He also appointed a Hindú, named Rái Alam Chand, to be Joint-Díwán of Bengal with his son Sarfaráz Khán; and procured for him the high title of *Ráy-Ráyán*. The new Nawáb also selected a Council of Four by whose advice he carried on all important measures of Government; two of these were relations of his who had lately migrated into Bengal from Dehli, two brothers named *Hájí Ahmad* and *Alí Virdí Khán*; the third member of Council was the Ráy-Ráyán; and the fourth was the great banker Jagat Seth.

During the first part of his reign Shujá-ud-dín appeared fully to deserve his good fortune; for he administered justice with great impartiality, and was singularly charitable and liberal, and distinguished also for his care for religion; but in his later days, he became indolent and luxurious. At first he carefully guarded the subjects from all oppression; and even executed Násir Ahmad [*see* § 23], who had been his predecessor's instrument in extortion. At the same time he was very careful to remit large sums of revenue to Dehli; and he also largely increased the army, maintaining 25,000 men instead of the four or five thousand with which Murshid Kulí Khán had governed. With all these expenses, and his own luxurious and liberal habits, he soon began to feel the want of money; and hence during his reign first commenced a system of supplementary taxation in addition to the taxation on land. This additional taxation was called *Abwábs*; and though, long before this, vast sums had been raised in this way, they had always been looked upon as the perquisites of the subordinate officers. The *Abwáb* revenue was publicly collected

CHAP. VI.] THE MUHAMMADAN RULE IN BENGAL. 73

for the Government for the first time in the reign of Shujá-ud-dín; and then amounted to nearly twenty-two lakhs in addition to the regular revenue.

[NOTE.—The *Abwábs* were fees on the renewal of zamíndárs' leases, *nazaránahs*, fees to maintain the Nawáb's elephants, and many more arbitrary exactions of the same nature. The *Abwábs* rapidly increased under Alí Virdí Khán and Kásim Khán; so that when the East India Company in 1765 acquired the Díwání, the total revenue of Bengal was more than two crores and fifty six lakhs of rupees.]

§ 25. *The Rise of Alí Virdí Khán.*—In the year 1729, the Nawáb appointed a member of his Council, the famous Alí Virdí Khán, to be Deputy-Governor of Bihár. Alí Virdí found the country in a great state of insubordination and disorder, the zamíndárs of Bhetiá in Champáran, and Bhojpur in Sháhábád, being in open revolt; so he took into his pay some Afghán troops under Abdul Rahím Khán, and by their aid suppressed all the bands of robbers, and subdued the refractory zamíndárs one by one. He forced the zamíndárs to pay him large sums in addition to all their arrears of revenue. After he had thoroughly settled the province, he found that his Afghán troops were inclined to be overbearing and insolent; so with no compunction or remorse he caused Abdul Rahím to be assassinated. This outrage confirmed his authority; but will always be a disgrace to his name.

§ 26. *Shujá-ud-dín continued; and his son Sarfaráz Khán.*— The most important events of the reign of Shujá-ud-dín were: (1) the conquest of Tiparah by Mír Habíb, the Díwán of Dacca, in 1732; this territory was now for the first time fully included in the Mughul Empire: (2) the abortive attempt of the Germans to establish an East India Company, called the Ostend Company, 1730—1734.

When Alí Virdí Khán was appointed Governor of Bihár, Shujá had wished to give the appointment to his son Sarfaráz Khán; but the young man's mother (who, as heiress of Murshid Kulí Khán, often took upon herself to meddle in affairs of State) refused to part with him. So Sarfaráz was at length appointed

Governor of Dacca; but a Deputy-Governor was also appointed, so that Sarfaráz might remain with his mother at Murshidábád; and a very able and popular Hindú, named Jeswant Rái, was appointed Díwán, and had the real charge of the administration in the province of Dacca. From the benevolent conduct and successful measures of his Díwán, Sarfaráz Khán obtained great credit for his government of Dacca; and especially for the fact that the district was so prosperous that rice was once more sold, as it was in the time of Sháistah Khán, at eight *mans* for the rupee—in consequence of which, Jeswant Rái ordered the gate that had been closed by Sháistah Khán [*see* § 17, *last paragraph*] to be again opened in 1735. But this prosperity was short-lived; for when Sarfaráz Khán made his own son-in-law Governor of Dacca, Jeswant Rái resigned his post, and the whole of the district soon sank into comparative poverty and desolation.

During the last years of Shujá's reign, Sarfaráz Khán had nearly the whole management of the State in his own hands; and he contrived at this time to offend many of the greatest men in the State, especially the councillor Hájí Ahmad, the brother of Alí Virdí Khán. When Shujá died, he nominated Sarfaráz as his heir; but with strict injunctions to attend to the advice of the Council, *i.e.*, of Hájí Ahmad, the Ráy-Ráyán, and Jagat Seth. But he had not been on the throne long before he grossly insulted Jagat Seth and disgraced his family, by insisting on being allowed to see the face of the beautiful wife of Jagat's eldest son. He also interfered in a marriage that had been arranged by Hájí Ahmad, and married the young lady to his own son. Jagat Seth and Hájí Ahmad now determined to depose the Nawáb; and accordingly entered into a conspiracy to set up Alí Virdí Khán, the Governor of Bihár.

The first step of the conspirators was to obtain a fresh patent from the Court of Dehli, appointing Alí Virdí to the government of Bengal as well as to that of Bihár; and this was easily obtained from the weakness of Muhammad Sháh, who had only just been reinstated after the conquest of Dehli by Nádir Sháh, King of Persia. They then induced the Nawáb to dismiss many of his troops; and all these soldiers were immediately sent up to Patná, where they were re-engaged by Alí Virdí. At length, all preparations being complete, the latter marched from Patná with his army—at first, ostensibly, against a refractory zamíndár —and even up to the last, with a pretence of being friendly to Sarfaráz Khán. But when Hájí Ahmad had been allowed to leave Murshidábád and join his brother under the excuse of a negociation, Alí Virdí suddenly fell on the army of the Nawáb; Sarfaráz Khán fought bravely, but his army was utterly routed and he himself killed. This battle was fought near *Gheriah*, about twenty-two miles north of *Murshidábád*, in the year 1740.

CHAPTER VII.

THE MUHAMMADAN RULE IN BENGAL. PART V.—THE NAWABS OF BENGAL NOMINALLY UNDER THE EMPEROR OF DEHLI, BUT REALLY INDEPENDENT.

§ 1. Settlement of Bengal by Alí Virdi Khán. § 2. Settlement of Orissa. § 3. The Mahratta Invasions of Bengal. § 4. Other events of the reign of Alí Virdí Khán. § 5. The Accession of Siráj-ud-daulah. § 6. The Massacre of the *Black Hole*. § 7. The defeat and death of Sakat Jang. § 8. The End of Siráj-ud-daulah.

§ 1. *Settlement of Bengal by Alí Virdí Khán.*—Alí Virdí Khán, whose character presented the unusual combination of valour and energy with prudence and even dissimulation, behaved with the utmost moderation after his victory over Sarfaráz Khán. He pretended the utmost submission to the old Begum Zainat-ul-nisá, the daughter of Murshid Kulí Khán and the mother of Sarfaráz. He transmitted immense presents to the Emperor Muhammad Sháh and the courtiers of Dehli; and when the Emperor was dissatisfied with these presents and sent Maríd Khán to demand the arrears of revenue, he induced Maríd by bribes to return to Dehli with some further presents without obtaining any settlement of the revenue. The three sons of Hájí Ahmad were married to their cousins the daughters of Alí Virdí; on these Alí Virdí now bestowed the chief offices in Bengal; and he adopted his grandson the son of Zain-ud-dín the youngest of the three brothers—a youth who is best known by the title obtained for him from the Emperor, Siráj-ud-daulah.

§ 2. *Settlement of Orissa.*—The brother-in-law of the late Nawáb Sarfaráz, by name Murshid Kulí Khán, had been appointed Governor of Orissa by his father-in-law the Nawáb Shujá-ud-dín; and with him was associated the able Díwán Mír Habíb, who had conquered Tiparah and annexed it to Bengal during the time that he was Díwán of Dacca [*see* Chapter VI., § 26]. Mír Habíb had been present with all the troops of Orissa at the battle of Gheriah, but had taken no part in it; and when victory declared for Alí Virdí, he immediately marched back to Orissa to his master Murshid Kulí. When Murshid Kulí refused to give up the government of Orissa, Alí Virdí marched against him; drove him out of the country, and made his own nephew Sayyid Ahmad (the second son of Hájí Ahmad) Governor. The imprudence and profligacy of this young man soon led to a rebellion, in which he was taken prisoner, and the son-in-law of Murshid Kulí Khán was enabled again to establish himself in Katak. But the vigour and determination of Alí Virdí suppressed this rebellion; and with some difficulty he succeeded in rescuing his nephew Sayyid Ahmad from his dangerous captivity.

§ 3. *The Mahratta Invasions of Bengal.*—Alí Virdí was in the midst of the festivities which celebrated his final conquest of Orissa, when he was startled by the news that a powerful army of Mahrattas, forty thousand strong, had marched from Barár to invade his dominions; and before he had any time to make preparations, he was again surprised by the news that the invaders, so swift were their movements, were within a few miles of his camp.

[NOTE.—The Mahrattas, a Hindú nation of western and west-central India, were at this time the greatest native power in India; and if they had been united, they would probably have succeeded to the Empire of

CHAP. VII.] THE MUHAMMADAN RULE IN BENGAL. 77

India which was then falling to pieces in the weak hands of the later Mughul Emperors of Dehli. The Mahratta power was, however, divided amongst a number of chiefs; who were even more jealous of each other than of their common enemies. The two chiefs with whom we are concerned in the History of Bengal, were : (1) Báláji Báji Ráo, the *Peshwá*, who ruled at Púna, and who was regarded as the head of the Mahratta confederation; and (2) *Raghuji Bhonslé*, who was Rájá of Barár. The armies of the Mahrattas were dreaded throughout Hindústán and the Dakhin, for their plundering propensities, and for the rapidity of the movements of their fine cavalry. Their habit was to sweep through the provinces of an enemy at a rapid rate, to collect as much plunder and do as much damage as possible, and to retreat before they could be engaged in a pitched battle. Sometimes indeed they would remain long in the country of an enemy, as they did in Bengal; but they always moved about rapidly from place to place, so as to elude pursuit and harass their enemy, whilst they invariably avoided a pitched battle.]

This first invasion of the Mahrattas occurred in 1741 ; and for the next ten years, the unfortunate inhabitants of Bengal endured the most terrible sufferings from these pitiless and rapacious enemies, who overran the province in at least five separate invasions, who never gave the country rest for many months, and who literally desolated the face of the land, leaving hardly a handful of rice, a head of cattle, or even a living being, in the territory through which they passed.

The first invasion was under the command of *Baskár Ráo*, one of the chief officers of Raghuji Bhonslé of Barár. The Mahrattas at the first attack surrounded the camp of Alí Virdí near Bardwán, captured all his baggage and treasure, and very nearly made him a prisoner. Mír Habíb, the Díwán of Orissa under Murshid, who subsequently had taken service under Alí Virdí, having been captured by the Mahrattas, joined their standard, and now became one of the most dangerous enemies of Alí Virdí. The Mahratta general gave him the command of a troop of horse ; and with these he hastily rode off and plundered Murshidábád, and was only driven away by the rapid approach of the Nawáb. The Mahrattas now obtained absolute possession for a time of the whole of Western Bengal ; but at last the Nawáb succeeded in defeating them in a great battle at *Katwá* (*Cutwa*) and finally drove them out of the province, 1742.

During the progress of this invasion, large numbers of the inhabitants of Western Bengal crossed the river Hugli, and took refuge in Calcutta: and the English in consequence solicited and obtained permission from the Nawáb to dig a ditch around the city for its protection. This work was commenced in 1742; but only half the circuit of the city was completed, as the English began to think that they need no longer fear an attack from the Mahrattas. This moat was always called " the Mahratta Ditch."

In 1743, Bengal was invaded both by Raghuji Bhonslé himself, and also by Báláji the Peshwá; but the Nawáb, by heavy bribes, induced the Púna chief to march against the Barár Mahrattas and drive them out of the country. Next year (in 1744) the latter returned under their old general Baskár Ráo; when Alí Virdí, with the blackest and most disgraceful treachery, invited the general and his chief officers to a conference near Murshidábád, and caused them all to be assassinated; after which he easily expelled the Mahratta army from the province.

Again and again did these bold and persevering marauders return and devastate the fertile plains of Bengal, and oppress and massacre its inhabitants; until at last in 1751, the Nawáb agreed by treaty to cede to them the province of Katak (Cuttack) and to pay them annually twelve lakhs of rupees as *Chauth* for Bengal. The deserter Mír Habíb was made governor of Katak, nominally under the Nawáb, but with orders to hand over its revenue yearly to the Rájá of Barár: and he was subsequently assassinated and the province brought fully under the Mahratta power. Only a small portion of the north of Orissa remained annexed to Bengal; and when the Díwání of Bengal, Bihár, and *Orissa* was ceded to the British in 1765, the grant of Orissa referred only to this small portion [see Chap. VIII., § 3, footnote; and Chap. IX, § 3].

[NOTE.—The Emperor Muhammad Shah had ceded to the Mahrattas in 1720, the " Chauth" or fourth part of the revenues of the Dakhin; and in consequence of this grant, the Mahratta leaders* claimed a similar percentage on the revenues of the other provinces of the Mughul empire.]

§ 4. *Other events of the reign of Alí Virdí Khán.*—The

CHAP. VII.] THE MUHAMMADAN RULE IN BENGAL. 79

happy result of this treaty was that Bengal at last obtained rest from its sufferings, which had been incessant for more than ten years; and the Nawáb was enabled to apply himself to the internal administration of the country. He induced the people to rebuild the villages which had been destroyed, and to cultivate the lands which had been deserted or depopulated, during the Mahratta invasions; and during the later years of his reign, the country enjoyed great prosperity, which was only disturbed in some parts by the atrocities of his young grandson Siráj-ud-daulah.

During the Mahratta invasions, Alí Virdí's government had been threatened at various times by no less than three serious rebellions. The first was that of Mustapha Khán, the Nawáb's commander-in-chief; he succeeded in plundering Rájmahall and in seizing the fortress of Munger, but was subsequently defeated and slain by Zain-ud-dín, the governor of Bíhár, who was the son-in-law of the Nawáb and father of Síráj-ud-daulah. In the next rebellion, however,—that of the Afghán troops of the Nawáb's army, under Shamsher Khán—Zain-ud-dín was slain by the rebels at a conference; his aged father also, Hájí Ahmad, was tortured to disclose his treasures, until he too expired; and all Zain-ud-dín's family and treasures, including his wife the daughter of the Nawáb, fell into the power of Shamsher Khán. The Nawáb however, with his usual bravery and success, soon afterwards engaged the rebels at *Barh* near Patna; and though a large force of Mahrattas was at the time in the immediate neighbourhood, he utterly routed them, slew their leaders, and rescued his daughter, 1749.

The third rebellion was a short-lived attempt of Siráj-ud-daulah, in 1750, to depose his grandfather; and was remarkable on account of the extraordinary fondness for his profligate grandson displayed by the foolish old Nawáb, who was far more anxious about the safety of Siráj than about the success of his own arms. Siráj was immediately forgiven, with every display of affection; although the insolent messages which he had sent to his grandfather ought to have convinced Alí Virdí of the utter worthlessness and shameful ingratitude of the young Prince.

During the remainder of Alí Virdí's reign, Siráj-ud-daulah was allowed to gratify his bloodthirsty and licentious tastes almost as he pleased. He procured the assassination of a large number of persons who had offended him; including Husain Kulí Khán and his brother, who had been the favourites of Siráj's uncle the Governor of Dacca.

Both the uncles of Siráj (who were at once the nephews and the sons-in-law of the Nawáb) died shortly before the death of Alí Virdí himself in 1756. One of them, Sayyid Ahmad, the Governor of Purniá, left a son named *Sahat Jang*, who was about as old as Siráj-ud-daulah; and he was the only person from whom the latter could anticipate any opposition in succeeding his grandfather.

Alí Virdí Khán was intelligent in all affairs; and made a point of encouraging the deserving in every line of life. He was affable in manners, a good and wise statesman, and a brave and skilful general. He always had a high regard for the English of Calcutta; and when urged by some of his officers to expel them, he is said to have remarked, " What have the English done against " me, that I should use them ill? It is difficult to extinguish fire " on land; but should the sea be in flames, who can put them out?" This he said, referring to the maritime power which he well knew the English possessed. In accordance with this opinion, he never interfered with the English trade; and though commerce was often injured by the depredations of the Mahrattas, yet Calcutta continued to flourish and increase during his reign.

§ 5. *The Accession of Siráj-ud-daulah.*—We have already seen that the young heir of Alí Virdí Khán had been so much indulged by his fond grandfather, that being naturally of a cruel and perverse temper, his vices ripened with his age. As he grew up, he associated only with infamous and profligate companions; and with these, he used to walk about the streets of Murshidábád and insult every person of respectability, male and female, whom he might meet.

Immediately after his accession he commenced oppressing his Hindú subjects in the most atrocious manner; degrading the noblest families of Bengal by his licentiousness, impoverishing them by his extortions, and terrifying them by his inhuman oppressions. But his first acts were directed against the relatives and friends of his grandfather the late Nawáb. He dispossessed his aunt, the widow of the late Governor of Dacca, of all the property she possessed; and turned her out of her beautiful palace called the *Mútíjhíl*, near Murshidábád. He next displaced his grandfather's chief officers; appointing in their room the base companions of his own debaucheries. Amongst the officers thus set aside was *Mír Jafar* the paymaster-general. He also endeavoured to seize all the wealth of Rájá Rájballabh, the deputy-governor of Dacca; but the latter contrived to send off his son Krishna Dás with his family and treasures to Calcutta.

Very soon a conspiracy was formed by all those persons whom the Nawáb had injured or insulted, to depose him and set up his cousin *Sakat Jang*, the son of Sayyid Ahmad and his successor in the government of Púrniá. Siráj-ud-daulah however got information of this conspiracy, and immediately set out with his army to punish his cousin; but before he got very far, he received letters from Calcutta which so enraged him that he altered his course and prepared to march at once and expel the English from the country.

§ 6. *The Massacre of the "Black Hole."*—During the reign of Alí Virdí Khán, the English at Calcutta had been growing very rich and prosperous; and in the years just preceding the elevation of Siráj-ud-daulah, the military abilities of a young officer named CLIVE had made the English name feared and respected throughout India, by his splendid victories in the Carnatic.

The independence of the English merchants of Calcutta had made them the objects of the special wrath of Siráj-ud-daulah; and his anger was now further inflamed by the reply of Mr. Drake to his demands that Krishna Dás (the son of Rájá Rájballabh) should be given up and the fortifications of Calcutta dismantled. Mr. Drake peremptorily refused to comply with either of these demands; in consequence of which the Nawáb returned with his army to Murshidábád, and proceeded to seize and plunder the Company's factory at Kásimbazár, near Murshidábád——taking as prisoners all the English officers, amongst whom was young Warren

Hastings, now twenty-four years of age. He then marched on Calcutta, where the English Council were altogether unprepared for such an attack. They tried in vain to conciliate the Nawáb; and in their distress asked help from the Dutch at Chinsurah and the French at Chandernagar, who only replied with a contemptuous offer of protection within the walls of the latter settlement. The Nawáb arrived before Calcutta on the 16th June, 1756; and after a slight check at the Mahratta Ditch, began to bombard the fragile defences of the English, who were soon driven within the walls of the fort. They now (18th June) held some hurried and disorderly councils; the women and children were sent on board one of the vessels in the river under the charge of two high officials; and at nightfall the Governor lost courage and went off to the ships in the last boat. The ships now weighed anchor and dropped down the river to Faltah, leaving the unfortunate soldiers and officers of the garrison to their fate.

The latter elected Mr. Holwell as their leader; who the following morning felt himself compelled to negotiate, and in the afternoon the Nawáb's army marched in. The Nawáb summoned Mr. Holwell to his presence, accused him of rebellion and of having concealed the treasures of the English factory; but promised him that no harm should happen to the prisoners. Notwithstanding this, the whole garrison, consisting of 146 men, were crammed into a small dungeon eighteen feet square, with very small apertures for light and air. This miserable dungeon, ever since infamous in history under the name of THE BLACK HOLE, had been used as a place of punishment for single individuals; and the torments now endured by the unhappy prisoners, during a night of the hottest season of the year, were more terrible than any thing that has ever been described. They endeavoured by alternate threats and bribes to induce their jailors either to put an end to their tortures by death, or to obtain better quarters from the Nawáb; but the miscreant Siráj was asleep, and the guards were (or pretended to be) afraid to awake him. At first the struggles of the victims for the places near the windows, and for the few skins of water that were handed in to them, were terrific; but the ravings of madness gradually subsided into the moans of exhaustion; and in the morning, only twenty-three wretched figures almost in the pangs of death, were extricated from a pestilential mass of dead bodies. It is uncertain whether the Nawáb was really an active accomplice in this wholesale murder; but in his anxiety to discover the treasures which he supposed the English had concealed, he took no pains to prevent it, and he evidently felt no subsequent remorse about it. He was morally responsible for it, and a terrible vengeance was justly inflicted on him.

§ 7. *The Defeat and Death of Sakat Jang.*—The Nawáb, after this fatal success which was to prove his ruin, marched back to his capital; but he first extorted 4½ lakhs from the Dutch at Chinsurah, and 3½ lakhs from the French at Chandernagar, by threatening to treat them as he had already treated the English. Shortly afterwards he gave orders for the release of Mr. Holwell, at the intercession of his grandmother the widow of Alí Virdí Khán; and then proceeded to test the intentions of his cousin Sakat Jang, by appointing an officer to a post under the authority of the latter, and ordering Sakat Jang to see that his wishes were carried out. Sakat Jang immediately sent back a defiant answer, claiming the government for himself, and offering Siráj-ud-daulah an asylum in Eastern Bengal; "but," Sakat Jang's letter continued, "do not presume to take with you any of the treasures or other valuables." Siráj-ud-daulah was enraged at this insolence; and immediately marched towards Púrniá. His officers were however so little pleased with his conduct, that Sakat Jang if he had been only moderately prudent must certainly have succeeded in conquering him. But the character of Sakat Jang was hardly, if at all, better than that of Siráj-ud-daulah; he was equally vain, cruel, and incapable of government; he delighted to humiliate all the old and experienced officers of his father, who were skilled in war; and as he would allow no one to command the army but himself, and he was utterly ignorant of war, no order or discipline was maintained. But even under these circumstances he might have gained the day, so strong was the hatred felt against Siráj-ud-daulah; but he insisted on giving the most foolish orders to his troops, reproached his officers with cowardice when they remonstrated with him; and when at last it was necessary that he should appear on his elephant in the battle to encourage the troops, it was found that he was so drunk as not to be able to sit erect. He was however held up by a servant; but he had not advanced far, before a ball struck him in the forehead and killed him on the spot. All his troops immediately took to flight. This battle was won at *Nawábganj* near Púrniá, in October 1756. The troops of Siráj-ud-daulah were led by Rájá Mohan-lál. The Nawáb himself had not ventured nearer to the scene of war than Rájmahall; and yet he assumed no little merit for this victory, and returned with great pomp and rejoicing to Murshidábád.

§ 8. *The End of Siráj-ud-daulah.*—The Nawáb had supposed that, by the capture of the fort and the destruction of the garrison of Calcutta, he had rendered his government secure and had expelled the English from the country; he little thought that his wicked and cruel conduct had brought upon himself the vengeance of an inveterate foe, which would result in his own shameful death and the transfer of the Government of Bengal to the hands of the English. The news of the disasters in Bengal soon arrived in Madras, and filled the settlement with consternation. But Colonel Clive and Admiral Watson were now at Madras, where they had arrived in triumph after the capture of Gheriah. They were soon ready to sail to avenge the massacre in Bengal, with 900 English troops and 1,500 Sepoys, all full of enthusiasm for the cause and of confidence in their leaders. Various delays however occurred; and they did not arrive in the river Hugli till December 1756. And now commenced in earnest the work of retribution; Budge-budge was taken, Calcutta occupied, and the town of Hugli stormed. At Budge-budge Warren Hastings (afterwards the great Governor-General) fought as a volunteer, and here he met Clive for the first time; Hugli was stormed by a young Captain named Eyre Coote, afterwards the conqueror of Lally and of Haidar. Such was the band of heroes who, with their little army, decided the fate of India. The tyrant Nawáb knew something of the wars in the

Carnatic, and had a lively dread of the defender of Arcot and the conqueror of Gheriah; hence after the recapture of Calcutta by Clive on January 2, 1757, he made pressing overtures for peace, offering to reinstate the English in their former position. The honest old Admiral Watson disapproved of any accommodation with the author of the Black Hole massacre, saying that the Nawáb should be "well thrashed;" but Clive from political motives agreed to sign the treaty, February 9, 1757.

Clive now seized the opportunity to humble the French in Bengal. Notwithstanding the opposition of the Nawáb, who aided the French with men and money, he attacked Chandernagar; and with the aid of Admiral Watson and the fleet, he captured the town in May 1757.

The Nawáb, filled with distrust and fear of the English, was intriguing with the Frenchman Bussy, who was now at Katak (Cuttack), which he had lately obtained for the French ; the English had learnt their power, and remembered the Black Hole; so it was obvious that the peace could not last long. Meanwhile, the Hindú subjects of the Nawáb had been goaded to desperation by his frantic excesses ; and a powerful conspiracy was set on foot against him, headed by Rájá Ráidurlabh, his treasurer, and Jagat Seth the richest banker in India—joined by Mírjáfar the Commander-in Chief, and many discontented Muhammadans. The English, represented by Mr. Watt, the resident at Murshidábád, entered into the conspiracy with alacrity; and it was felt by Clive, and indeed by all the Council at Calcutta, that Siráj-ud-daulah must be crushed if the English settlement wished for peace and security. The conspirators agreed that Mírjáfar should be set up as Nawáb in the place of the tyrant; and that the English should receive from the gratitude of Mírjáfar ample compensation for all their losses and rich rewards for their assistance.

Umáchand, a crafty Bengáli, was the agent employed to transact business between the English and the Nawáb ; and he was an active helper in the plot. But at the last moment he threatened to turn traitor and disclose all to the Nawáb, unless he were guaranteed a payment of thirty lakhs (£300,000). Clive and the other conspirators were in despair ; and at last they condescended to cheat Umáchand, in order to escape from their present difficulty. Two copies of the treaty between the English and Mírjáfar were made out; one on white paper was the real treaty, in which no mention was made of Umáchand's claims; the other, on red paper, a mere fictitious treaty, in which Umáchand was guaranteed all the money he demanded, was shown to the faithless Bengáli. This piece of deception has always been a stain on Clive's character; Admiral Watson (who had already shown himself to be an honest English gentleman in objecting to a temporizing policy with the Nawáb) refused to sign the false treaty—so his signature was forged by the others.

Clive now wrote in peremptory terms to the Nawáb, demanding full redress of all grievances, and announcing his approach with an army to enforce his claims; and immediately afterwards set out from Chandernagar, with 650 European infantry, 150 gunners, 2,100 sepoys, a few Portuguese, and 10 guns. the Nawáb's army consisted of 50,000 infantry, 18,000 cavalry, and an immense train of artillery. As Clive approached the Nawáb's encampment near Kasimbazár, Míjráfar appears to have lost courage; for he ceased to communicate directly with the English, whilst it was known that he had taken solemn oaths to his master, that he would be faithful to him. Under these alarming circumstances, Clive called together his officers in a Council of War, to decide whether they should fight against such enormous odds, or should wait for a better opportunity. The majority of thirteen, including Clive himself, voted for the latter course; only seven, at the head of whom was Eyre Coote, voted for immediate fight. After dismissing the council, Clive took a solitary walk in an adjoining grove; and after an hour's solemn meditation, he came to the conclusion that Coote was right, and that the attack ought to be made at once. Accordingly, early next morning he crossed the river with his little band, and came upon the Nawáb's army about daybreak in the fields and groves of PLASSEY. During the early part of the day the English remained almost entirely on the defensive; contenting themselves with repelling the charges of the enemy's cavalry, and keeping up a desultory cannonade. At length, however, some of the Nawáb's chief officers having fallen, the troops of Mírjáfar (who had hitherto remained undecided) were seen to separate themselves somewhat from the rest of the Nawáb's army; Clive now gave the order for a general charge and carried all before him. Siráj-ud-daulah mounted a swift camel; and escorted by 2,000 of his best cavalry, fled to Murshidábád. The great battle of Plassey, which virtually transferred the sovereignty of Bengal (and ultimately of India) to the English, was fought on June 23, 1757; the victors only losing 22 killed and 50 wounded.

Mírjáfar, now that the English were successful, openly joined Clive; who did not condescend to notice his vacillation, but saluted him Nawáb of Bengal, Bihár, and Orissa. Siráj-ud-daulah fled in disguise from Murshidábád, and the victors at once occupied that city. The fugitive was soon betrayed by a Hindú whose ears he had formerly cut off. He was seized and brought before the new Nawáb. Mírjáfar wished, or pretended to wish, to spare him; but his son Míran caused him to be put to death. And now came the settlement of the engagements of the treaty. Vast sums were paid to the Company, to the British merchants, and to the Native and Armenian merchants of Calcutta as indemnity for their losses in the sack of the city. The army and the navy with their leaders, including Clive, Watson and the members of Council, all shared in the spoil. Umáchand expected, too, to get his thirty lakhs, but he was soon undeceived. He was at first stunned by the blow; but he seems to have recovered, for he was afterwards recommended by Clive as " a person capable of rendering great services, and therefore not wholly to be discarded."

CHAPTER VIII.
THE ENGLISH RULE IN BENGAL. PART I.—FROM THE BATTLE OF PLASSEY, 1757, TO THE REGULATING ACT, 1774.

§ 1. Clive's first Administration. § 2. Vansittart and Spencer, successively Governors of Bengal. § 3. Clive's second Administration. § 4. Verelst, Cartier, and Hastings successively Governors of Bengal. § 5. The *Regulating Act*, 1773-4.

§ 1. *Clive's First Administration.*—Clive was now virtually ruler of Bengal, Mírjáfar being a mere tool in his hands. He was made Governor of the Company's settlements and fortresses, and remained at the head of affairs until 1760.

The new Nawáb soon displayed the utmost ingratitude and jealousy towards those of his subjects who had been the leaders in the conspiracy by which he had obtained the throne, and especially towards the Hindús. Rájá Ráidurlabh the treasurer, Rájá Rám Náráyan (who had long been deputy-governor of Patna), Rájá Rám Singh the Governor of Midnapore, and Rájá Adit Singh who had been appointed to succeed Sakat Jang as Governor of Púrnía—all experienced the hatred of Mírjáfar; and in several cases a reconciliation was only effected by the mediation of Clive himself.

In 1759 the new Nawáb was terribly frightened by an invasion of Alí Gauhar, now called the Emperor Sháh Alam II. Alí Gauhar had fled from Dehli whilst his father Alamgir II. was under the power of one of his usurping nobles called Ghází-uddín; and inasmuch as Alamgír had made him titular Súbahdár of the eastern provinces, he crossed the Karmanása (between Oudh and Bihár) to obtain possession of his rights, at the very time that his father was murdered by Ghází-ud-dín. He did not receive the news of this murder for a whole month; he then assumed the title of Emperor, and appointed the Nawáb of Oudh his Vazír. The Governor of Bihár, a Hindú named Rám Náráyan, was defeated by the imperial troops, and shut himself up in Patna.

Clive promised Mírjáfar and Rám Náráyan that he would help them; and immediately sent off Colonel Calliaud with some troops, who soon defeated the forces of the Emperor and the Nawáb of Oudh, in the (first) battle of Patna, 1760. The Emperor now wrote to Clive asking for his help; and the latter at once sent him some money on condition that he left the province of Bihár without delay. This Sháh Alam consented to do; and Mírjáfar, in gratitude for his deliverance, presented Clive with the revenues due to him from the Company, as a *jágír*.

About the same time it was discovered that the Dutch at Chinsurah were intriguing with the faithless Mírjáfar, to help him to rid himself of his powerful English masters. Clive immediately attacked the Dutch by sea and land, besieged them in Chinsurah, and compelled them to submit to the most humiliating terms. He now sailed for England, 1760; and did not return until 1765. He was received with the greatest honour by the King, by the great prime minister Pitt, and by the whole nation; and was raised to an Irish peerage as Lord Clive.

§ 2. *Vansittart and Spencer, successively Governors of Bengal.*—Mr. Vansittart, an utterly incompetent man, succeeded the great Clive as Governor in Bengal. The Nawáb was hopelessly in arrear in the payments which he was pledged to make to his English protectors; and was evidently actuated by no very friendly feelings towards them. He was madly extravagant in his expenditure; and since the death of his son Míran, who had been killed by lightning in the Patna campaign, his affairs had got into worse and worse confusion. At length he sent his son-in-law Mír Kásim to Calcutta, to arrange matters with Mr. Vansittart and the Council; the latter were struck with Mír Kásim's ability, and resolved to dethrone the Nawáb and put his son-in-law in his place. The plan was carried out. Mírjáfar was induced to resign, and to take up his residence in Calcutta; and Mír Kásim, as the price of his elevation, ceded to the British the three districts of *Midnapur, Bardwán, and Chittagong.* This was in 1760.

Mír Kásim began with great energy to carry out reforms. He reduced expenditure* and paid off his English friends; and, disgusted with his position, resolved to shake off their yoke. He removed his capital to Munger, and there quietly gathered together and disciplined his army. This he did with surprising judgment and skill. His conduct on the whole was vigorous and just; but he was cruel in his treatment of Rám Náráyan the Governor of Patna, whom he despoiled. One of the worst features in the administration of Mr. Vansittart, who was con-

---

* By increasing the *Abwáb* revenue enormously [*see* Chap. VI., '§ 24, *note*] he raised the revenue to a total of Rs. 25,624,223.

tinually quarreling with his Council, was his failure to protect Rám Náráyan.

About this time Sháh Alam II., who dared not return to his capital, was hovering about Bihár with a lawless host. Colonel Carnac attacked and dispersed them in the second battle of Patna; and Law, the Frenchman, was taken prisoner with his band, and to the surprise of the natives treated with great courtesy. The Emperor himself was persuaded by Carnac to join him, and accompany him to Patna; where Mír Kásim was induced to pay him homage, and was in consequence formally invested with the Súbahdárship of Bengal, Bihár, and Orissa.

A quarrel between the Nawáb and the Calcutta Council soon arose. The cause was the immunity from the payment of transit duties claimed by the servants of the Company. This freedom had been formerly granted by Imperial Farmán to the Company itself [see Chap. VI., § 17]. It was now grossly abused. All the servants of the Company traded largely on their own private account; and they claimed freedom from the payment of all inland duties for themselves, their servants and dependents. Every native in fact, hoisting the English flag, could evade the payment of all duties. The Nawáb was defrauded of his revenues. His servants were insulted and the trade of the country was thrown into confusion. After attempts at a compromise, the Nawáb in desperation resolved to put his subjects and the English upon an equal footing, by abolishing all transit dues throughout his dominions. War ensued. Some English boats were stopped and examined by the Nawáb's officers at Patna. Mr. Ellis, the resident, rashly began hostilities and seized the city of Patna; but his European soldiers got drunk and the Native Commandant recaptured the city. Mr. Ellis and the other Englishmen were taken prisoners. The Nawáb even ordered every Englishman in his dominions to be seized. The Calcutta Council was resolved to dethrone Mír Kásim and reinstate Mírjáfar. A severe struggle ensued; and at Gheriah a battle was fought, which lasted for four hours, and in which the Nawáb's well-trained and disciplined troops showed most determined bravery, and were with difficulty overcome. This was in August 1763. Munger was soon after taken; and the Nawáb had only Patna remaining in his power.

Hitherto there had been little to blame in the conduct of Mír Kásim, which had been spirited, though his cause was a hopeless one. But the MASSACRE OF PATNA, 1763, the account of which we must now give, marks him as a man to be branded with perpetual infamy. On the approach of the English, he became desperate; he cast Rám Náráyan into the river with weights around his neck; and caused the Seths, the great bankers who were friends of the English, to be flung from one of the bastions into the river. He then declared his intention of murdering all his English prisoners, the moment their friends advanced to the attack of the city. The officer in command of the English forces sent a letter to the prisoners, asking them if they could suggest any means of releasing them. Their reply was a magnanimous one:—"There is no hope of escape; never mind us; do not delay the advance of the army one hour." The army moved on to the attack, and the ferocious Nawáb fulfilled his threat. He ordered his officers to kill all the Europeans in prison; but they nobly replied, "No! turn them out and we will fight with them, but not massacre them." But an executioner was found. A German, who had been a serjeant in the French service, and now held a commission in the Nawáb's army under the name of Sumru or Sombre, volunteered to do the bloody deed. He led a file of soldiers to the house, fired on the unarmed men through the windows: and soon forty-eight English gentlemen (Mr. Ellis among them) and 100 soldiers, were lying in their blood on the floor.

The English troops advanced, and took Patna after a vigorous resistance (November 1763); and Mír Kásim fled to Shujá-uddaulah, Nawáb of Oudh, with whom was Sháh Alam the Emperor of Dehli. The three now advanced on Patna, but were repulsed by the English army; and they then took up their position at Baxar on the Son.

And now took place the *first* Sepoy mutiny in the Bengal army. Major Munro acted with firmness. A whole battalion attempted to desert to the enemy. They were brought back, and twenty were blown away from guns. This firmness and promptitude at once crushed the mutiny. In October 1764, Munro led his troops against the Nawáb Vazír, who was still encamped at BAXAR with an army of 50,000 men. The latter was routed, and 160 pieces of cannon taken. The consequences of this victory were very great. The Nawáb of Oudh, long master of the empire, was humbled; and it thus made the English supreme in Hindústán. The emperor himself came to the British camp, and opened a negotiation with the Council at Calcutta for his restoration to the throne. It was reserved for Clive to reap the full fruits of this victory [*see* § 3].

The Calcutta Council, during the five years' absence of Clive, had fallen into a state of utter corruption under Vansittart and Spencer; and thought of nothing but enriching themselves. Mírjáfar died in January 1765, partly of vexation at their harassing demands. His son, a youth of twenty years of age, named Názim-ud-daulah, was put on the throne; the Council received large sums from him, and had the virtual control of the country. The Directors of the East India Company had at first hesitated about sending out Clive again, as he declined to go, unless full powers, independent of the Council, were entrusted to him. But at length they perceived the importance of the crisis, and the impossibility of proper administration without a man of Clive's energy and resolution; so he was at last sent out, May 1765.

§ 3. *Clive's second Administration.*—Clive's first measure was to enforce the orders of the Directors prohibiting the acceptance of presents by their servants. He made all sign covenants binding themselves to obey this rule.

Clive then proceeded to the English army which was at Alláhábád, where the Emperor Sháh Alam and Shujá-ud-daulah the Nawáb of Oudh, were suppliants in the camp of General Carnac. The result of his negotiations was that Oudh was restored to Shujá on condition of his being a faithful ally of England; the districts of Korah and Alláhábád were given to the emperor: and the latter conferred on the English the DIWANI (*i.e., the Office of Diwán* (really involving the whole sovereignty) of

CHAP. VIII.] THE ENGLISH RULE IN BENGAL. 93

Bengal, Bihár, and Orissa,* in return for a yearly payment of 26 lakhs. Though the English had long virtually possessed all the power thus given to them, the Imperial grant of the *Diwání* was valuable, as constituting them the legal (as well as the actual) sovereigns of the country. This happened on the 12th of August 1765. The Nawáb of Bengal was soon compelled to retire on a large pension.

The army had been accustomed to what was called *double batta* when on service. This was nominally an allowance of subsistence-money; but the amount was unreasonably great. Clive was instructed to stop this anomalous system. He was met by a combination of the European officers; which, in fact, was a mutiny. Two hundred officers agreed to resign in a single day; and as the Mahrattas were advancing, they thought themselves necessary to the State. Clive accepted each resignation, and put the ex-officer in immediate arrest; while he sent to Madras for every available man. Clive's firmness subdued the mutiny in a fortnight. His next contest was with all the services of the Company; the members of which universally were engaged in trade, which their position made especially lucrative, and which injured their character, while it prevented them from doing their duty as public servants. They were now absolutely forbidden to engage in any species of trade, and a compensation was granted.

Clive left India for the last time in 1767, a poorer man than he was when he returned to it in 1765. He was received in England with great honour; but his reforms had raised up for him a host of enemies. All whom he had punished, or whose corrupt schemes he had thwarted, leagued against him. The Court of Directors did not support him as it ought to have done; but a resolution was passed, " that he had rendered meritorious services to his country." He died in 1774.

---

* When Alí Virdí Khán ceded the Province of Katak to the Mahrattas, it was agreed that the river Súnamukhí (now called the Burhábalang) which flows by Balasor, should be the boundary between the Mughuls and Mahrattas. This was the boundary till 1803, when the English in the second Mahratta War conquered and annexed the whole province.

§ 4. *Verelst, Cartier, and Hastings successively Governors of Bengal.*—From 1767 to 1772, Mr. Verelst and Mr. Cartier were Governors of Bengal. From the grant of the *Diwání* in 1765, to the accession of Warren Hastings in 1772, Bengal was under what was called a "double government," *i.e.*, the actual administration of the country was in the hands of the Nawáb's servants, whilst the European officials vied with them in making haste to become rich by every species of corruption. The Governor in vain strove to stem the torrent. The Muhammadan Government had been destroyed; and no vigorous English rule had been substituted. The constitution of the Home Government of India was equally vicious. The Directors were appointed but for one year, and their chief anxiety was to make the most of their patronage. It was a period of unblushing jobbery and corruption.

The excuses that have generally been offered for the English officials in Bengal, are—that their salaries were shamefully small and insufficient, that they were consequently obliged to embark in private trade, that they were engrossed in this private trade, and (above all) that they knew nothing whatever of the system on which the land-revenue was levied. Muhammad Rezá Khán had been appointed Díwán of Bengal, and Rájá Sitábráy, Díwán of Bihár; the former lived at Murshidábád, the latter at Patna, and kept all knowledge of revenue matters to themselves.

The same defects that were evident in the administration of the revenue, were even more glaring in the administration of justice. This branch of the Government was nominally still in the hands of the Nawáb Názim; and the power of the English authorities, being nominally restricted to *Diwáni* affairs, did not extend beyond the limits of Calcutta in *faujdári* or police matters. A frightful increase of crime, and the enactment of the most severe and even cruel regulations to repress it, were the natural consequences of this state of things; and the affairs of Bengal only began to mend when the East India Company resolved in 1772 to abolish the Double Government, and to assume the direct management of the province through their own civil servants.

[NOTE.—The sufferings of the unfortunate people of Bengal during this period of anarchy were increased by a most terrible famine which occurred in the year 1769-1770, owing to the failure of the usual rains. Whole districts were depopulated, and vast numbers of villages were actually left silent and deserted. It has been computed that one-third of the whole population of Bengal died of starvation or disease resulting from insufficient food.]

WARREN HASTINGS was appointed in 1772 Governor of Bengal by the Directors of the East India Company, for the special purpose of effecting the great reform known as the *abolition of the Double Government.* Hastings was now forty years of age; and for the next thirteen years, from 1772 to 1785, the history of British India is the history of this great man. He had already distinguished himself greatly in various high and important posts in the Bengal civil service; he had given valuable evidence about Indian affairs before the English Parliament; and he had been a Member of Council at Madras. He was now sent as President or Governor to Calcutta; which was now made the seat of the Díwání, instead of Murshidábád.

Hastings immediately issued a proclamation, declaring that the East India Company, as Díwán, would henceforward take the management of the revenues into its own hands, through its Civil Servants called *Collectors;* and he also sent out a Committee, consisting of four Members of Council, to go throughout the land, and effect a revenue-settlement for five years with the landholders. The Díwáns of Bengal and Bihár, Muhammad Rezá Khán and Rájá Sitábráy, were put on their trial for malpractices; and the former, though acquitted, was not allowed to return to the public service. Rájá Sitábráy, however, was not only honourably acquitted, but he was also presented with a "Dress of Honour" by the Council, to compensate him for the humiliation which had been inflicted on him. He was also declared Ráy Ráyán of Bihár; but all these honours came too late, for the high-spirited old man could not brook the indignities that had been offered him, and he died soon after of a broken heart.

Warren Hastings also without delay made new arrangements

for the administration of justice. He established two Courts of Civil and Criminal justice in each district; and two Courts of appeal in Calcutta, the *Sadar Diwáni Adálat* for appeals in civil cases, the *Sadar Nizámat Adálat* for appeals in criminal cases. A new code also was drawn up without delay.

[NOTE.—In 1775, the *Sadar Nizámat Adálat* was moved back to Murshidábád, and again put under native management only—Muhammad Rezá Khán was put at its head as *Náib Názim*, or deputy of the Nawáb. All this was again finally altered by Lord Cornwallis in 1790; when the Sadar Nizámat Adálat was again brought to Calcutta, and was ordered to consist of the Governor-General and the Members of the Supreme Council, aided by the chief native law officers. At last Lord Wellesley in 1801, finding it impossible that the duties could be adequately discharged by the Governor-General and Members of Council, determined that they would give up both the *Sadar Diwáni Adalat* (as Warren Hastings had done, see Chap. IX., § 1) and the *Sadar Nizamat Adalat*; placing the chief civil and criminal jurisdiction in the hands of three Judges, called the Sadar Court. The Sadar Court remained as the final Court of Appeal until 1862, when it was joined with the *Supreme Court* [see § 5] to form the present High Court.]

§ 5. *The Regulating Act,* 1773-1774.—Meanwhile the affairs of the East India Company were still involved in the most utter confusion; for the conquests of Clive and the large increase of territory had been glorious but not profitable, as the expenses incurred had been enormous. The financial distress of the Company, and the accounts that had been received in England of that bad administration in India of which we spoke in the last section, induced the English Parliament to enquire carefully into the conduct of English subjects in India, and to consider the whole question of the Government of India. The consequence was that an Act of Parliament was passed to regulate the Government of India; it was called the *Regulating Act*, and came into operation in 1774, though it had been passed in 1773. It laid down some wise laws about the appointment of the Directors of the East India Company in London; its most important provisions immediately affecting India were the following:—

(1.)—That the Governor of Bengal should henceforth be the

Governor-General; and, *with his Council*, should be supreme over all the British possessions in India.

(2.)—That a Supreme Court of Judicature should be established in Calcutta, consisting of a Chief Justice and two other Judges, all barristers, appointed by the English Ministers of State and independent of the Company. It was intended that this Court should only have jurisdiction over the city of Calcutta, and in cases in which Englishmen were concerned.

In consequence of this Act, Mr. Hastings became Governor-General of India, as well as Governor of Bengal, in October 1774.

CHAPTER IX.

THE ENGLISH RULE IN BENGAL. PART II.—THE GOVERNORS-GENERAL OF BRITISH INDIA AS GOVERNORS OF BENGAL.

§ 1. Warren Hastings. § 2. Lord Cornwallis. § 3. Lord Wellesley. § 4. The Conquest of Orissa by the British. § 5. Lord Cornwallis, a second time Governor-General; Sir George Barlow; Lord Minto. § 6. The Marquis of Hastings. § 7. Lord Amherst. § 8. Lord William Bentinck. § 9. Lord Auckland. § 10. Lord Ellenborough. § 11. Lord Hardinge. § 12. Lord Dalhousie. § 13. Conclusion.

§ 1. *Warren Hastings.*—Warren Hastings was the first man who, under the *Regulating Act*, performed at the same time the functions of Governor of Bengal, and those of Governor-General of the whole of British India. It must of course be remembered, in reading this Chapter, that many great and important events occurred in other portions of India under the jurisdiction of the Governor-General, which will not be mentioned here, because we are only concerned with those things which happened in Bengal itself. And in accordance with this, it must also be remembered that, although the events we have to describe here are concerned only with the peaceful administration of the country—for with hardly any interruption, Bengal has enjoyed profound peace ever since the battle of Plassey—yet the Governors of Bengal, in their capacity as Governors-General of India, have been almost always engaged in great wars, have fought great and famous battles, and have made great conquests. But after all, no part of India does more credit to the British name, than Bengal; for the triumphs of peace are more important and more honourable than those of war; and the gratitude of a happy and prosperous people well governed, is far more valuable than the empty glory that is gained by extensive conquests.

Warren Hastings became Governor-General, with his Council of four, in October 1774. The provision of the Regulating Act, by which the members of the Governor-General's Council were invested with equal power in Council with himself, soon proved to be destructive of all good government. The first members of Council were Mr. Francis (afterwards Sir Philip Francis), Colonel Monson, General Clavering, and Mr. Barwell. Francis soon displayed the most bitter hostility against Hastings and all his measures; and was supported by Monson and Clavering, thus forming a majority in the Council. Barwell, who had long served in India, supported Hastings; but the latter was unable successfully to contend against the factious opposition of the other three, until the death of Monson in 1776.

The people during this interval generally regarded the power and authority of Hastings as extinct; and many accusations were brought against him by persons who wished to please the factious majority in the Council. Of these charges the most serious were brought forward by Nandakumár, a man infamous for his treachery and perfidy; Francis and his colleagues, however, took him under their protection and encouraged him in his charges against the Governor-General. Suddenly Nandakumár was arrested, at the suit of an eminent native merchant, for forgery; he was tried by Sir Elijah Impey, in the Supreme Court, was found guilty by a jury, and hanged—hanging was at that time the usual punishment for forgery. This execution of a Bráhman created a great sensation, and Hastings has often been accused of having procured it unjustly to screen himself; but there seems no reason to doubt that Nandakumár was justly condemned to death. Good proof that Hastings was in no way concerned with the conviction and execution, is to be found in the fact that the members of Council might have interfered to refer the matter to England; but they refused to do so.

The Judges of the Supreme Court established in Calcutta, in striving to "protect natives from oppression and give India the benefits of English law," committed many great mistakes. They interfered between the zamíndárs and their ráyats. Their attorneys stirred up strife everywhere. Hastings interfered to protect the landholders from this vexatious interference, and Parliament was petitioned for a change of system; and meanwhile a remedy was discovered. In the *Sadar Diwání Adálat*, the Governor-General himself and his Council were appointed to preside. This they could not do; and Hastings offered the appointment of Chief Judge of this Court to Sir Elijah Impey, the Chief Justice of the Supreme Court. This reconciled all parties, and enabled Impey to turn his attention to the subject of the administration of justice according to such forms as might suit the great simplicity of native habits. This, though disallowed by the Court of Directors at the time, is the system now restored by the amalgamation in each presidency of the Supreme Court with the Company's old Court of Appeal.

The settlement of the land revenue in 1772 had been for five years; and the experience of these five years proved that the assessments of the amounts payable by the various zamíndárs had been made without sufficient knowledge of the circumstances. The revenue got frightfully into arrear, nothwithstanding the fact that the Government remitted large sums; and many influential zamíndárs were irretrievably ruined. So when a new settlement had to be made in 1777, it was determined that a fresh settlement should be made every year, with a due regard to the circumstances of the zamíndárís at the time when each settlement should be made. The disadvantages of this system were, (1) that no zamíndár could know exactly the value of his land, because of the variable amount of the government rent; and (2) that the zamíndárs had little inducement to improve their estates, for they were afraid that the improvement might result in an increased demand for rent from the Government. We shall see that the system was altered by Lord Cornwallis a few years later

During the later years of his reign, Mr. Hastings adopted some harsh measures to obtain money for the many wars in various parts of India in which the British Government was involved. Many of these measures, especially those by which he obtained money from Chait Singh, Rájá of Banáras, and from the Begums of Oudh, were strongly condemned by the Directors of the East India Company; so Hastings signified his intention of retiring. He addressed letters to all the chiefs and princes of India, taking leave of them; and resigned with dignity a trust which he had held, first as Governor of Bengal, afterwards as Governor-General, for 13 years. He left India in February 1785. In England, he was received with favour by the King, the Ministry, and the Directors. But Pitt had a prejudice against him, though he extolled and even vindicated him. Francis, his rancorous foe, was in Parliament. The renowned orator Burke and the Whig party in general combined against him, and it was resolved to impeach him for his conduct in India. His trial before the House of Lords began on the 13th February 1788; and was protracted till the 23rd April 1795, when he was completely and honourably acquitted. The trial cost him 100,000*l*. Though thus reduced to comparative poverty, he lived peaceably at Daylesford till his death in 1819. Once only did he again appear in public, and then he was called to give, in 1813, evidence before the House of Commons regarding Indian affairs. On that occasion the whole assembly stood up to do him honour.

Some important alterations were made by the English Parliament in 1774, in the constitution of the Government of India both in England and in this country. The chief point was that the control of the British Indian empire was confided in all essential points, to a Minister of the King of England, who was called President of the Board of Control; who had the power of appointing the Governor-General. The Act of Parliament that made these alterations was called Pitt's India Bill.

The names of two Englishmen who occupied important positions in Bengal during the Governorship of Mr. Hastings, deserve to be mentioned here. *Mr. Cleveland* was the Magistrate in charge of the district of Bhágalpur; and he devoted his life to the civilisation and improvement of the condition of the poor aboriginal tribes so numerous in that district [see Chap. I., § 3]. His health was ruined by the bad climate of the hills and jungles amongst which he laboured, and he died at sea on his way to England; but the natives of his district showed their gratitude to him by erecting a monument to his memory. The fame of *Sir William Jones* depends not so much on his philanthropy—though he too was distinguished for his zeal for the improvement of the natives of this country—as on his devotion to all branches of Indian literature, and especially to the cultivation of Sanskrit learning. He was the founder of the *Bengal Asiatic Society*, a society of English and native scholars devoted to the study of oriental science and literature.

After the departure of Mr. Hastings, Sir John Macpherson, senior Member of Council, acted as Governor-General, and Governor of Bengal, for twenty months, from February 1785 to September 1786; and at length Lord Cornwallis was appointed by the Indian Minister of the King of England to take his place.

§ 2. *Lord Cornwallis.*—Lord Cornwallis arrived in Calcutta in September 1786, and remained until 1793. His administration was firm and vigorous, and greatly consolidated the British Indian Empire; which, founded by Clive and Hastings, was strengthened and reduced to order by Cornwallis. His great energies were at first directed to the removal of corruption from all branches of the public service. At this time small salaries were given to the Company's servants; and as their opportunities were great, they easily yielded to the temptation of enriching themselves by every species of official depredation. His first real measure of effectual reform was assigning to every officer of Government such a salary as should leave him no shadow of excuse for trading, or attempting to acquire money by corrupt practices. This measure, added to an incomparable firmness and consistency in resisting all jobbery and favouritism, and in punishing all frauds, soon caused the purity of the Indian services to become as conspicuous as their corruption had been notorious.

Lord Cornwallis obtained great glory from his successful wars;

but the chief ground of his fame was the *Permanent Settlement* which he effected of the revenues of Bengal. The Directors of the East India Company had in 1786 written out to India orders that all engagements for the payment of revenue ought to be made directly with the zamíndárs. Lord Cornwallis issued a series of enquiries on the subject throughout; and made a settlement with the zamíndárs at first for ten years—at the same time promising that the settlement should be declared a permanent one, if it were found to be on the whole satisfactory. Opinions differed very widely as to whether the settlement ought to be made permanent; but at length, in 1793, Lord Cornwallis, with the consent of the Directors, declared it to be permanent. By this measure the zamíndárs were assured that they would always be maintained in the possession of their lands, provided they regularly paid a fixed sum annually to the Government as rent; and in this way they were encouraged to improve their estates, by the knowledge that the fruits of all improvements would be secured to themselves. It appears however that the rights of some classes of ráyats were not sufficiently protected from the encroachments of zamíndárs, owing to the fact that the English officials were very generally uncertain about the exact nature of these rights.

The reform of the Civil and Criminal Courts of Bengal next occupied the attention of Lord Cornwallis. We said above that Sir Elijah Impey, when he was put at the head of the Sadar Díwání Adálat, devised some rules for the administration of justice in a way suited to the habits of the people of India. These rules were now developed into a book of Regulations by Sir George Barlow; and the system of Civil Courts and procedure, which with modifications still exists, was established. The greatest evil of this system was the power it gave to the police of oppressing the people. Natives were excluded from all share in the administration of justice, and from all but the most subordinate public offices. This was remedied in after times.

Lord Cornwallis left India in October 1793, after a most successful administration. He was succeeded by Sir John Shore (afterwards Lord Teignmouth), a civilian who had obtained great praise for his able conduct of affairs in the preparations for the Permanent Settlement; of which measure, however, he had been an opponent. His five years' administration was marked by no event of importance.

§ 3. *Lord Wellesley.*—The Marquis Wellesley arrived in India as fourth Governor-General, May 1798, and left in August 1805. He was a man of real genius, a good scholar and a great statesman; his administration was more brilliantly successful than that of any other Governor-General.

At the moment of his arrival, the British empire in India was threatened by a combination of a large number of native chiefs, who were encouraged to resist the English arms by the aid and the money of the French, with whom the English had now been long at war. Tippú, the powerful Sultán of Mysor, the Nizám of Haidarábád, and Sindia the most powerful of the Máhratta chiefs, were all under French influence, and had their armies chiefly officered by Frenchmen; whilst Zamán Sháh, the Durráni monarch of Afghánistán and the Panjáb—the grandson of the terrible Ahmad Sháh Abdáli who had so often overrun Hindústán—threatened to invade Northern India as an ally of Tippú Sultán. But Lord Wellesley, by his extraordinary vigour and ability, soon dissipated all these dangers. He expelled the French officers from every part of India; he overawed the Nizám and Sindia; and finally he took by storm the great fortress of Seringapatam, the capital of Mysor, the cruel Tippú Sultán being slain in the battle. By the conquest of Mysor, the British power became unquestionably paramount in the Dakhin, A.D. 1799.

After this, a short interval of peace enabled the Governor-General to attend to some internal reforms [*see* the note on the history of the *Sadar Court*, page 96] and to establish some useful institutions. Amongst the latter may be mentioned the College of Fort William in Calcutta; which was intended to instruct the young members of the Civil Service in the languages and literature of India. An important result of this foundation was a largely increased cultivation of the Bengáli language; followed by the diffusion of a desire for education amongst the natives of this country, which began to bear fruit a few years later, in the time of the Marquis of Hastings.

One of the subjects of continual debate during this administration was the question of allowing *private trade* to India. The Company in 1793 allowed 3,000 tons annually for this purpose; but the trade of private individuals soon passed this limit. Lord Wellesley wished to throw the trade open, and thereby incurred the displeasure of the Directors. In 1802, the Court reduced various items of expenditure sanctioned by the Governor-General, removed Mr. Webbe the able Secretary of the Madras Government, and interfered in such a vexatious way with the prerogatives of the Governor-General, that the latter intimated his intention of returning to England that year. Lord Clive, the Governor of Madras, son of the great Clive, resigned in consequence; and was succeeded by Lord W. Bentinck. The Governor-General, however, was induced to remain another year; and that year fixed the destinies of British India; it was the year of the Second Mahratta War.

In this war the power of the Mahrattas was completely broken by the British—mainly owing to the great military talents of the brother of the Governor-General, General Wellesley, who afterwards became the great DUKE OF WELLINGTON. In the battle of *Assai*, 1803, Sindia and the Rájá of Barár were totally defeated by General Wellesley, and forced to run away from the field; and before the end of the year all the Mahratta dominions, including Dehli and Agra and the person of the Mughul Emperor, had fallen into the hands of the English.

§ 4. *The Conquest of Orissa by the British.*—The parts of the Mahratta dominions nearest to Bengal were those under the power of the Rájá of Barár; for ever since the treaty of 1751 between Alí Virdí Khán and the Mahrattas [see Chap. VII., § 3], the whole of Orissa except the small tract north of Balasor had been under the Barár Rájá.

[NOTE.—The poor Uriyás had suffered great oppression from their Mahratta conquerors, as may be seen from the following description of the Mahratta taxation:—The taxes levied in different places varied with the idiosyncrasies of the Government or of the individual tax-collector; but

CHAP. IX.] THE ENGLISH RULE IN BENGAL. 105

among them it may be noticed that people were mulcted for having houses to live in, or, if they had no houses, for their temporary sheds or huts. If they ate grain, their food was taxed at every stage in progress through the country; if they ate meat, they paid duty on it through their butchers. When they married, they paid for beating drums or putting up marquees. If they rejoiced at the set Hindu festivals, they paid again: at the "holi," for instance, on the red powder which they threw at each other; at the "páña," on the ornaments which they tied to the horns of their cattle. Drinkers were mulcted by an excise, and smokers by a tobacco duty. Weavers, oilpressers, fishermen, and such low caste industrials, had as a matter of course to bear a special burthen. No houses or slaves or cattle could be sold, no cloth could be stamped, no money could be changed—even prayers for rain could not be offered, without payment on each operation of its special and peculiar tax. In short, a poor man could not shelter himself, or clothe himself, or earn his bread, or eat it, or marry, or rejoice, or even ask his gods for better weather, without contributing separately on each individual act to the necessities of the State! These were the regular taxes merely, and it certainly does not seem likely that any money could have slipped by owing to their want of comprehensiveness; but the revenue accounts of the times show that supplementary measures were occasionally found necessary to reach men who would otherwise have escaped.]*

As soon as the campaign between General Wellesley and the Mahratta chiefs commenced, the Governor-General sent an army from Madras into Orissa under the command of Colonel Harcourt; who entered Púrí without opposition on the 18th September 1803, and having left a guard of English soldiers to protect the sacred temple of Jagannáth, passed on to Katak (*Cuttack*). The town of Katak capitulated on the 10th of October; and its fortress was taken by storm three days later. Meanwhile a detachment of Bengal troops from Calcutta took possession of Balasor and the northern portion of the province; and the two armies, joined under the command of Colonel Harcourt, soon completed the conquest of Orissa, 1803-1804.

Towards the close of the year 1804, a serious insurrection broke out amongst the Uriyás themselves. The chief Rájá of the Uriyás, the Rájá of Khurdah, was a descendant of the old

---

* This account is taken from Toynbee's *History of Orissa*.

Hindú kings of the country. During the rule of the Afgháns and Mughuls, his ancestors had been the most powerful zamíndárs in Orissa, and were regarded as semi-independent princes, only feudally subject to the Muhammadan rulers. Though the Mahrattas had taken away all that part of his territory which lay in the plains and which therefore was accessible, he had still maintained a sort of independence in his mountain strongholds. As soon as the British had driven out the Mahrattas, the Rájá of Khurdah tendered his allegiance to the new conquerors; but in the following year, 1804, being displeased, because Colonel Harcourt did not give him back the lands formerly taken from him by the Mahrattas, he foolishly ventured to rebel. He was immediately defeated, captured, and confined as a prisoner in the fort of Katak.

The great Lord Wellesley left Calcutta in August 1805, after a glorious and successful administration. He had largely extended the British dominions in India; and though the Directors of the East India Company did not approve of his policy, yet they praised him for his " ardent zeal to promote the well-being of India, and to uphold the interest and honour of the British Empire." They granted him a sum of £20,000 ; and placed his statue in the India house.

§ 5. *Lord Cornwallis, a second time Governor-General. Sir George Barlow; and Lord Minto.*—That party in England which was opposed to the bold policy of the great Marquis Wellesley, succeeded in obtaining the appointment of Lord Cornwallis as his successor ; and the latter arrived in Calcutta for the second time, August 1, 1805. He came to India pledged to reverse the policy of Lord Wellesley, and to bring about an immediate peace with the Mahratta chiefs, Sindia, and Holkár at any cost. He condemned the treaty of Bassein ; and was proceeding to join Lord Lake at the seat of war with the intention of insisting on a peace, when he died at Gházipur.

The senior member of Council, Sir George Barlow, succeeded to the Governor-Generalship, and was bent on carrying out the peace policy of Lord Cornwallis. He was however soon superseded ; and Lord Minto, who had been Viceroy of Corsica, and subsequently President of the Board of Control, was sent out to India in his place. Sir George Barlow was made Governor of Madras.

The administration of Lord Minto was not marked by any important events in Bengal; though he soon found it impossible to avoid all interference with Native States, and was indeed compelled frequently to interfere in the affairs of the Mahrattas and others. He returned to England in 1813. He was made Earl of Minto; but he died in the same year. His name has always been respected as that of one of the ablest rulers of British India.

In 1793, the East India Company's Charter had been renewed for twenty years. The time had now come for the reconsideration of the subject. The result was the destruction of the Company's monopoly, for which the Court of Directors made a determined struggle. The trade to China was still to remain in their hands, but the trade to India was thrown open.

§ 6. *The Marquis of Hastings*, 1813—1823.—The Earl of Moira (afterwards the Marquis of Hastings) was appointed to succeed Lord Minto; and arrived in Calcutta in October 1813. He found the finances embarrassed, and many disputes with Native States pending; for nine years he ruled with resolution and success, and left the Empire in a flourishing condition. He was a distinguished soldier, an experienced statesman, and a man of amiable manners and noble character. During his reign of nine years, Lord Hastings was chiefly engaged (1) in a war against Nepal, (2) in settling the affairs of the Mahrattas, who as well as the Pindáris* were at this time finally reduced to submission. A band of Pindáris threatened Orissa in 1816, but were dispersed by some English troops from Madras.

Subsequently, in 1817, a formidable insurrection broke out in Orissa, under a brave and clever Uriya named *Jagabandhu*, who

---

* The Pindáris were hordes of lawless predatory freebooters, that had followed like jackals the armies of the early Mahratta Chieftains, by whom assignments of land had been made to them on the banks of the Narbaddah.

was the hereditary *Bakshi* (or *paymaster of the forces*) under the Rájá of Khurdah [*see* last section]. This man had been treated unjustly by the English officers after the conquest of Orissa in 1803 ; and now, instead of complaining of his grievances in the English Courts in a lawful manner, he put himself at the head of a disorderly band of *paiks*,* and actually succeeded in capturing the town of Púrí; but the rebellion was soon suppressed, and its leader driven into the jungles of Central India. Jagabandhu was a man of gigantic size and strength ; and in a temple at Khurdah there is still shown a large rock of 225 cubic feet in content, which he partially raised from the ground on one occasion when he was scratching his back against it. After this insurrection had been put down, bands of paiks continued to infest the jungles of Khurdah for some time, acting as dacoits, and often murdering inoffensive subjects; at length, in 1818, they were regularly hunted down by the British sepoys, and Orissa has ever since enjoyed profound peace.

The arms of Lord Hastings were successful in all parts of India and a great portion of this vast country was brought under the British power; at the same time this truly great Governor used his utmost exertions to promote the cause of civilisation and education amongst the people committed to his charge. Under his encouragement, a great College was founded in Calcutta and called the Hindú College; and this was the origin of the Presidency College. Lord Hastings also warmly encouraged the cultivation and diffusion of vernacular literature; and the first Bengáli newspaper appeared during his reign, and was allowed by him to be circulated through the post at a very cheap rate.

---

* The *Paiks* or zamíndárí militia of Orissa (*Sipáhí Zamíndárí*) were soldiers who performed military service to their chiefs in return for assignments of land (*see* the note on *Jágírs* at page 43). The war dress of the Paiks consisted of a cap and vest made of the skin of the tiger or leopard, a sort of chain-armour for the body and thigh, and a girdle formed of the tail of some wild animal. They further heightened the ferocity of their appearance by staining their limbs with yellow clay and their countenance with vermilion. These men had often fought bravely for their chiefs both against the Mughuls and against the Mahrattas.

The Marquis of Hastings returned to England in 1823, accompanied by the applause of all.

§ 7. *Lord Amherst*, 1823—1828.—Lord Amherst was appointed to succeed the Marquis of Hastings; Mr. Canning having been offered and having declined the nomination. Mr. Adam acted as Governor-General until the arrival of Lord Amherst in August 1823, and made himself very unpopular by imposing some severe restrictions on the press.

The arrogance of the Burmese, whose territories had lately been extended through Arakán and Assám to the frontiers of Bengal, had long threatened to bring them into collision with the English. In 1818, the King of Ava made an impudent demand for the cession of some of the eastern districts of Bengal, as part of the ancient kingdom of Arakán; which demand was, of course, treated with contempt. In 1823, the Island of Sháhpúri was occupied by thirteen sepoys, for the protection of British subjects. A body of a thousand Burmese expelled them. Kachár was next attacked, and British troops were sent to aid the fugitive Rájá. It was now determined to invade Burmah, and bring the King of Ava to his senses.

Sir Archibald Campbell commanded the expedition, which comprised both Bengal and Madras troops; and sailed to the mouth of the Rangoon river in May 1824. Great difficulties were experienced on account of the heavy rains, and the defective commissariat arrangements. Many successes, however, were obtained, and many battles gained; the most noted Burmese general named Mahá Bandula being killed at the capture of Donabu early in 1825. Town after town was taken; and at the battle of Pagahn in the following year (1826), two thousand British troops routed a Burmese army of 18,000. After this the English prisoners, were released; and the negotiations for peace, which had been twice broken off by the obstinacy of the King of Ava, were renewed.

At length when the English army had reached Yendabú, only four miles from the capital, a treaty was signed; by which the King of Ava agreed to resign all claims to Assám, Kachár, and Jaintiá, to cede Arakán and several other rich provinces, and to pay a crore of rupees as a partial indemnification for the cost of the war.

A mutiny occurred among the sepoys at Barrackpur, in connexion with this war. The 47th regiment of native infantry, feeling aggrieved at some trifling hardships to which they were temporarily subjected, broke out into open mutiny. Sir E. Paget, the Commander-in-Chief, hastened to the spot, surrounded the mutineers, and on their obstinately refusing to submit, caused a battery of artillery to fire upon them. They fled at once; and some who were taken prisoners were executed. The number of the regiment was erased from the list of the army.

After the annexation of Assam and Kachár by the treaty of 1826, the British officer who had formerly been called the Commissioner of the north-east Frontier, was made Commissioner of Assam, and put under the Government of Bengal. But it was only by degrees that a regular administration was established there. Upper Assam was granted in 1833 to Rájá Purandhar Singh as a tributary, and similar engagements were entered into with the chiefs of several tribes; but gradually the whole of the country was regularly settled under a British administration; and in 1837 a Code of rules for the administration of Assam was put forth by the Sadar Court with the sanction of Government.

In 1826, the fortress of Bhartpur was stormed by the English army under Lord Combermere, who was Commander-in-chief under Lord Amherst. The only importance attached to this conquest was owing to the fact that many of the enemies of the English rule in India had believed, or pretended to believe, that Bhartpur was such a strong fortress that even the English could not take it.

In 1827, Lord Amherst went to Dehli, and solemnly informed the King of Dehli (the representative of the old Mughul Emperors, who at this time was in receipt of a pension from the British Government) that the English were now the paramount Power in India. Up to the period of this declaration, the representative of the Mughul Emperors had been regarded as nominally the Lord Paramount of India, though his power had long before really passed into the hands of the British.

Lord Amherst, one of the least eminent of the rulers of British India, retired in March 1828 ; and Mr. Butterworth Bayley, one of the distinguished school of statesmen trained under the Marquis Wellesley, acted as Governor-General unti the arrival of his successor.

§ 8. *Lord William Cavendish Bentinck*, 1828—1835.—Lord William Bentinck had formerly been Governor of Madras; and he had been recalled in 1807. He was consequently anxious to have a chance of retrieving his reputation, by becoming Governor-General of India; and he fully attained the object of his wishes, for his administration marks an era of peaceful improvement and progress in India. It commenced in July 1828, and lasted until March 1835; and though not remarkable for any great military exploits, was distinguished by a large number of reforms, economical, judicial, and social, of the greatest value and importance.

Many important economical reforms were carried out by Lord William Bentinck in the civil and military administrations. Of these the one that provoked most opposition was the abolition of *double batta*. *Double batta* is an allowance given to the army when on service, in addition to their ordinary pay. The judicial reforms carried out at this time were of considerable importance ; especially with reference to the extended employment of native judicial officers in responsible posts.

But the reform for which Lord William Bentinck is most famous, was the abolitition of *sati* or *suttee*. This horrible custom (the self-immolation of widows on the funeral pile of their deceased husbands) had long been practised in India, though by many scholars it was believed not to be authorised by the Sástras. The Governor-General, aided by Mr. Butterworth Bayley and Sir Charles Metcalfe, his two councillors, at this time (December 1829) enacted that any person aiding or abetting a *sati* should be visited with the terrors of the law. The barbarous superstition is now nearly obsolete in India.

In 1829, the Governor-General appointed Major Sleeman (afterwards Sir William Sleeman) as Commissioner for the suppression of *thuggee*. The *thugs* were bands of wretches, half-robbers and half-fanatics, who were in the habit of decoying away and murdering unprotected travellers, especially in the forests of Central India. This occupation was at once their religion and their mode of subsistence. The active efforts of Major Sleeman and his coadjutors fortunately resulted in the almost total suppression of the crime.

Thomas Babington Macaulay (afterwards the famous Lord Macaulay) was the law member of Council in Calcutta from 1835 to 1840. It was chiefly owing to his influence, that at this time the oriental system of education was displaced by the European system in Government educational institutions. The exclusive use and study of the English language was somewhat modified at a later time, under Lord Auckland. It was seen that the great impulse to native education must be given through the medium of English, as the key to all modern science. It is for native scholars who have received a high English education to revive and enrich their own vernacular literature; and thereby to render possible a wholesome system of education for the masses of India, who can only be reached through the vernacular languages.

About this time was established steam communication between India and England, by the *overland route* through Egypt and the Red Sea. Rámmohan Rái, a distinguished Bengáli scholar and reformer, visited England as an agent of the titular King of Dehli; and died at Bristol in 1833.

At the renewal of the Company's Charter in 1834, its commercial character was altogether taken away, the monopoly of the trade with China being now abrogated. The Company thenceforward existed only as a ruling body. At the same time Agra was made the capital of a fourth Presidency, and Sir Charles Metcalfe appointed the first Governor; but in 1835, this was again changed, and the North-Western Provinces have remained ever since under a Lieutenant-Governor. The Governor-General in Council became Governor-General of India; but as Governor-General of Bengal, ruled this province without a council.

Lord William Bentinck left India in May 1835; and Sir Charle Metcalfe took his place as acting Governor-General, until the arrival of a successor in March 1836. Under Metcalfe, who was supported by the advice of Macaulay, all vexatious restrictions on the free action of the press were removed.

§ 9. *Lord Auchland, 1836—1842.*—Lord Auckland, who was appointed to succeed as tenth Governor-General of India, arrived in Calcutta in March 1836, and ruled until March 1842. His administration is chiefly famous for the melancholy disasters of the Afghán war; in which a large number of British soldiers perished, and which spread a gloom over British India, until the brilliant successes of General Pollock and the conquest of Kábul under the next Governor-General (Lord Ellenborough) restored the glory of the British arms. During this reign, the excellent measures of Lord Hastings and Lord William Bentinck were gradually bearing fruit in Bengal; and though no public events of great importance occurred in this province, its peaceful progress was most remarkable, and a large number of able and patriotic Native gentlemen were receiving the benefits of an education which they have since used in the good work of educating and civilising their countrymen.

In 1838, the sanitarium of Dárjiling was ceded by the Rájá of Sikkim.

[NOTE.—Some more territory was taken from the Rájá of Sikkim in 1850, as a punishment for imprisoning a British Officer. Subsequently in 1865 a war was undertaken against the inhabitants of Bhután, to punish them for some misconduct; a considerable tract of territory, called the Bhután Dwárs, was taken from them, and annexed to the British district of Dárjiling.]

Lord Auckland retired in March 1842. The disasters of the Afghán war, authorised by him, have clouded a reputation which would otherwise have been an honourable one. His abilities were great; and before the commencement of the war his good management had placed the finances of the country in a most flourishing condition.

§ 10. *Lord Ellenborough, 1842—1844.*—Lord Ellenborough, who had been President of the Board of Control [*see* § 1], was appointed to succeed Lord Auckland; and arrived in Calcutta in February 1842. His general administration of the government of India is chiefly famous for (1) the avenging expedition into Afghánistán under General Pollock, which conquered Kábul and punished its inhabitants for their former resistance, and then evacuated the country; (2) the conquest of Sindh; and (3) a short war with Gwáliár, which effectually put a stop to the turbulence of that State. Lord Ellenborough had many quarrels with the Directors of the East India Company; and at length he was suddenly recalled by them in August 1844.

§ 11. *Lord Hardinge,* 1844—1847.—Sir Henry Hardinge, afterwards Viscount Hardinge, was appointed to succeed Lord Ellenborough. He arrived in Calcutta in 1844, and left it in 1847. He had served with distinction under the Duke of Wellington in the Peninsular war and at the battle of Waterloo, where he lost an arm. The chief events of his administration are connected with the First Síkh War; but we shall here have to notice some important social reforms carried out by him, particularly the suppression of infanticide and of human sacrifices amongst some aboriginal tribes.

After all the great and bloody wars, in which the armies of Sindh, of Gwáliár, and of the Síkhs had been successively annihilated, India enjoyed peace for nearly two years; and Lord Hardinge was able to apply himself to those humane efforts for the suppression of cruel customs, with which his name is honourably connected. The horrible crimes of thuggee, infanticide, *sati*, and human sacrifices were still prevalent in many parts of India. Of the last the most important were the *Meriah* sacrifices in Gumsar, amongst the Khands and other aboriginal tribes of Orissa, Gondwána, and the hills and forests of Central India. These were now suppressed, chiefly by the efforts of Captain Macpherson and Colonel Campbell.

Free trade was at this time promoted by the abolition of *octroi* duties, that is, of taxes paid for importing food and other merchandise into some of the large towns of India.

Lord Hardinge left Calcutta early in 1848. During his short administration he had gained the affections of all classes; and his name will always be remembered with respect as that of a skilful and gallant soldier, and a no less able and beneficent politician.

§ 12. *The Earl of Dalhousie*, 1848—1856.—The Earl of Dalhousie was appointed to succeed Lord Hardinge as thirteenth Governor-General. He arrived in Calcutta early in 1848, and left it in 1856. The most important events of his administration were connected with (1) the Second Sikh War; (2) the Second Burmah War; (3) the annexation of Oudh; (4) the reversion of the States of Tanjor and Nágpur to the British; (5) considerable improvements in the material prosperity, especially aided by the introduction of railways and telegraphs.

When Lord Dalhousie was appointed, it was with the hope that he would be able to secure peace for India after the late terrible wars. But the turbulence of the Síkhs soon rendered the maintenance of peace impossible. When the news of the outbreak in the Panjáb arrived in Calcutta, and Lord Dalhousie had determined that there must be another Síkh war, he made the following famous speech:—" I have wished for peace; I have longed for it; I have striven for it. But if the enemies of India desire war, war they shall have; and on my word, they shall have it with a vengeance."

The result of the war thus begun was the annexation of the fine country of the Síkhs called the Panjáb; and this acquisition of territory was followed, during the reign of Lord Dalhousie, by the addition of Pegu in Burmah, of Oudh, of Nágpur, and of Tanjor, to the British Empire in India.

And now we come to the time when Bengal was given a Government of its own, separate from the general Government of India, though of course subordinate to that Government. The English Parliament was occupied during several months of 1853 in the consideration of the renewal of the East India Company's Charter; and amongst many other important changes made at this time, it was ordered that Bengal should be put under a Lieutenant-Governor. Mr. Halliday, an eminent Bengal civilian, now Sir Frederick Halliday, being the first Lieutenant-Governor. The jurisdiction of the new Lieutenant-Governor was declared to be co-extensive with that of the former Government of Bengal, with the exception of the Burmese provinces which were retained under the direct authority of the Government of India. At the same time the Civil Service of India was thrown open to public competition; and the old Company's Sadar Courts were combined with Her Majesty's Supreme Courts at the Presidency towns, and named "High Courts" [see note, page 96].

Before leaving the account of Lord Dalhousie's administration, we should observe that it was marked by a wonderful degree of material, social, and political progress. The first Indian railway was opened in 1853; and railways and telegraphs began rapidly to spread over the whole country. Vast schemes of education were set on foot; Universities were ordered to be founded, and the Presidency College in Calcutta was established in 1855. Gigantic schemes of public works were planned, and large sums of money borrowed for them; and the crime of extracting evidence by torture was stringently put down. Lord Dalhousie left Calcutta on the 6th of March 1856. His administration had been a singularly vigorous and brilliant one, and had lasted eight years. His health was utterly broken down by his labours and anxieties; but his fame will always endure as one of the greatest of the Governors-General of British India.

§ 13. *Conclusion.*—With the establishment of the Lieutenant-Governorship of Bengal under Sir Frederick Halliday in 1854, we shall close this brief survey of Bengal history; for the events of subsequent years are too recent to be fitly recorded in a book of this nature. We may however simply mention a serious insurrection of the Santáls, which was put down in 1855, and which led to some salutary measures for ameliorating the condition of the poor and rude aboriginal tribes of Bengal; and to the war with Bhután in 1865, which led [see note, page 113] to the annexation of a portion of the Dárjiling district.

Sir John Peter Grant succeeded Sir Frederick Halliday in 1858; and he was followed by Sir Cecil Beadon. Sir William Grey succeeded on the retirement of Sir Cecil Beadon; Sir George Campbell succeeded Sir William Grey. Early in the year 1874, the present Lieutenant-Governor of Bengal, the Hon'ble Sir Richard Temple, K.C.S.I., entered on his high and important office.

Under the six great Statesmen whose names have been here thus briefly given, Bengal has vastly improved in every possible way. Education has been largely extended and greatly improved; in a primary form it has been extended to vast masses of the poorer classes; whilst in its highest form it has been so much improved, that some of our Bengáli gentlemen are amongst the most learned men in the world, and many of them are authors and scholars of no mean repute. Bengáli literature is rapidly increasing and improving; and the vernacular press has expanded in the most wonderful way.

The cultivation of Science, though not hitherto so successful as that of Literature, has also made great strides of late years. The Medical College of Calcutta, founded by Lord William Bentinck, is now the largest Medical School in the world; and the benefits of a scientific and humane system of medicine and surgery are thus rapidly being diffused amongst the millions of Bengal. Railways, telegraph lines, and finely-made roads and tanks, are covering the whole country; and large numbers of native Engineers, and other scientific men, are every year sent out from the Government schools, and are able to use their knowledge in the patriotic task of developing the resources of their country.

Whilst Literature and Science have thus flourished, the wealth of the country has increased at an equal rate. Commerce has been fostered in every conceivable way; and new and scientific methods of agriculture, and of manufacturing jute, cotton, and the other products of the soil, have been introduced, and promise to make Bengal one of the richest countries in the world. Every endeavour has been used by the benevolent Government to make the life and property of all subjects perfectly secure; and most valuable reforms in the judicial system have from time to time been effected, with the view of giving cheap and speedy justice to all. In every way the rulers of Bengal have tried, and successfully tried, to prove to the world that the great object of the Government is the happiness of the people. That the people of this country may be happy and prosperous, has been often declared, and is well known, to be the ardent wish of Her

Gracious Majesty Queen VICTORIA, who is Empress of India as well as Queen of England; and the same kind feelings inspire His Excellency the Viceroy of India, and His Honour the Lieutenant-Governor of Bengal, who are the rulers more immediately set over us, by the Divine Providence, in this land. We cannot conclude this little book better than with the expression of a hope, that the same Divine Providence that has given us a good and benevolent Government, may at all times guide our Rulers to such measures as may best conduce to the true welfare of the country.

www.ingramcontent.com/pod-product-compliance
Lightning Source LLC
Chambersburg PA
CBHW020122170426
43199CB00009B/592